HOW TO BUY MUTUAL FUNDS
THE SMART WAY

STEPHEN LITTAUER

Dearborn
Financial Publishing, Inc.

Publisher: Kathleen A. Welton
Associate Editor: Karen A. Christensen
Senior Project Editor: Jack L. Kiburz
Interior Design: Lucy Jenkins
Cover Design: Salvatore Concialdi

Published by Dearborn Financial Publishing, Inc.

Printed in the United States of America

93 94 95 10 9 8 7 6 5 4 3 2 1

Library of Congress Cataloging-in-Publication Data

Littauer, Stephen L.
    How to buy mutual funds the smart way / by Stephen Littauer.
        p.   cm.
    Includes index.
    ISBN 0-79310-478-5 : $16.95
    1. Mutual funds—United States.   I. Title.
HG4930.L57   1993
326.63'27—dc20   92-29645
                                                                         CIP

To my wife Susan

The plans of the diligent lead to profit
as surely as haste leads to poverty.

—Proverbs 21:5

C O N T E N T S

PART THREE   Mutual Fund Strategies

PART FOUR   Tax-Advantaged Retirement Plans for Your Business

APPENDIXES

INTRODUCTION

NOTHING IS FREE: THE PRICE IS TIME, EFFORT OR MONEY

There is a price for investing in mutual funds. As an investor, however, you can choose how to pay that price. The easiest way is to pay a sales commission to a broker (account executive) of anywhere from 4 percent to 8.5 percent of the funds you wish to invest. On a $10,000 investment, the broker would be paid from $400 to $850, leaving you with a net amount invested of $9,600 to $9,150.

A different price you can pay is in your own time and effort by obtaining and reading basic information about mutual funds. The results can be that you will pay *no* commissions to anyone, the full amount of your investable funds will be working for you and very likely you will end up with a more profitable investment.

The reasons you can do better on your own are simple. First, it is easy for you to buy directly from mutual fund companies without going through a salesperson. Second, brokers are probably no smarter than you are. Third, *you* are more concerned about your money than anyone else. And fourth, brokers are paid to sell and will tend to push whatever is currently "hot" (not necessarily good) and pays them the best commission.

This book has been written for the many people who already own mutual funds, for those planning to invest in mutual funds and for those who simply believe the time has come to undertake a sound investment program.

Since World War II the financial world has witnessed a virtual explosion in the growth of mutual funds. Today there are more than 40 million shareholder accounts, with invested assets totaling over $1 trillion! Why has there been so much growth? Mutual funds provide an easy solution to the major problem confronting investors: how to attain diversification, professional management and liquidity at reasonable cost and in the investable amounts they have available. Even institutions such as pension and university endowment funds, which can afford to pay for private money managers and know about the alternatives, invest in mutual funds.

This book will especially help the financial do-it-yourselfer, the person who likes to be in control, reduce costs and rely on his or her own judgment. Such a person wants to take the initiative and is willing to do the research and deal directly with the mutual funds of his or her choice. He or she would prefer not to be guided by a salesperson, wondering if the recommendations are in the investor's best interests or serve the interests of the salesperson.

Many longtime owners of mutual fund shares are very pleased with the results and benefits they enjoy. Owners of stock funds have seen substantial growth in the value of their holdings. Similarly, many bond fund owners have experienced consistently high monthly dividends, while the value of their principal has held steady.

Other shareowners have had negative results. Certain stock funds have not only shown no growth but have significantly declined in value over the years. Some bond funds have also declined in value and have compounded the injury by reducing their dividend distributions.

There is no way to remove risk from the marketplace. The word *guarantee* is seldom heard in the lexicon of mutual funds, but the best way to achieve successful investing is for the investor to be informed. It is toward that end that this book has been written.

PART ONE

Information about Mutual Funds

CHAPTER 1

First, Some Background

At an increasingly rapid pace, mutual funds have come to have an important and in some ways dominant place in the financial world. They have become the investment of choice for millions of investors, and with good reasons, which will be discussed later.

But where did they start? In a somewhat different form, the origin of modern-day mutual funds dates back to the early 19th century, when they enjoyed substantial popularity in England and Scotland. Investment trusts, as they were then called, reached the United States in 1924, when the Massachusetts Investment Trust was organized. It was the first open-end mutual fund. During those early years, investment trusts were subject to various abuses and were brought into considerable disrepute.

Some of today's mutual fund giants were first organized in the 1930s. But the greatest growth of mutual funds occurred after World War II and has continued to this time with only occasional pauses. In 1946 mutual fund companies managed just over $2 billion in assets. By 1956 this had grown to $10.5 billion and to more than $39 billion in 1966. Growth became sluggish in the 1970s but then exploded in the 1980s, jumping from $64 billion in 1978 to more than $1 trillion by the end of 1991!

WHAT IS A MUTUAL FUND?

The basic idea of a mutual fund is simple. It is an organization whose only business is the proper investment of its shareholders' money, generally into stocks or bonds or a combination of the two (and more recently into money market instruments), for the purpose of achieving specific investment goals. To do this, it attracts funds from many individual and institutional investors, and it undertakes to invest and manage those funds more effectively than the investors could do on their own.

The ability of a mutual fund to accomplish its goals successfully depends first on how well it can invest a large amount of money into a diversified portfolio of securities that will meet its investment objective. In addition, it must manage its costs efficiently, provide continuous professional management over its extensive investment portfolio and lastly, provide the many services that mutual fund shareholders have come to expect.

Like other corporations, a mutual fund company issues shares of its own stock. Each share represents the same proportionate interest in the account (portfolio of securities) as every other share. After deduction of necessary expenses, income from the account is distributed to shareholders in the form of dividends. Investment profits and losses are reflected in the value of the shares. Realized profits are distributed to shareholders in the form of capital gains distributions.

One of the great benefits an investor gets by purchasing shares of a mutual fund is that the company's professional investment management and advisory services work for the investor.

OPEN-END AND CLOSED-END MUTUAL FUNDS

The most common and widely known mutual funds are the *open-end* funds. They have no fixed number of shares outstanding. The number of shares fluctuates from day to day because, for the most part, the funds are constantly selling new shares to investors, and they also stand ready to redeem outstanding shares from investors on any business day.

During a period when investors are buying more shares from a fund than are being redeemed, a cash balance will develop that must be invested, causing the fund to go into the marketplace to purchase securities. On the other hand, when investors are redeeming more shares than are being bought, the fund will be forced to sell securities to make cash available.

The value of an open-end mutual fund share is determined at the end of every business day. This is done by ascertaining the total market value of all the stocks, bonds and other financial instruments held in the fund, subtracting any liabilities and then dividing the balance by the total number of shares outstanding. This results in the *net asset value* (NAV) per share. When shares are offered for sale, the buyer will always pay the NAV per share (plus any sales charge that may apply) on the day of his or her purchase. In the same way, when a shareholder tenders shares for redemption, he or she will always receive the NAV per share (less any redemption charges that may apply).

Closed-end funds do not continuously offer new shares for sale, nor do they stand ready to redeem shares from shareowners who wish to sell. Instead, closed-end fund shares are sold in one initial public offering, like the shares of stock in any other corporation. They are then listed for trading on a national securities exchange such as the New York Stock Exchange. If an investor wishes to buy or sell shares, the investor does so by placing his or her order through a registered securities broker.

While the NAV of closed-end mutual fund shares are calculated in the same way as those of open-end funds, the price an investor will pay or receive for shares traded on an exchange may be above or below the NAV. This is because the price of the shares is determined on an auction market basis, the same as for all other traded shares of stock. Thus, the investor has an additional risk that the owner of open-end funds does not have. The value of his or her investment is subject not only to the fluctuations of the underlying securities in the fund itself but also to the fluctuating price of his or her shares on the exchange.

Managers of a closed-end fund have an advantage over their open-end peers, however. Since they do not have to worry about the uneven flow of money going in and out of open-end funds (resulting from share purchases and redemptions), their investment management decisions can be based entirely on economic and market conditions.

SUMMARY

With well over $1 trillion in assets, the mutual fund industry has become a dominant force on the national financial scene. Much of the daily trading activity in the organized stock markets is done by the funds. The idea of a mutual fund is to pool the money of many investors into a single investment portfolio that is then managed to achieve a stated objective.

There are two basic types of mutual funds. Open-end funds continually offer new shares to the public, while always standing ready to redeem the shares of investors who want to liquidate their holdings. Closed-end funds are sold in an initial offering to the public, and then the shares trade on an organized stock exchange, where investors buy and sell shares at prices determined by the auction market. Mutual funds provide an exceptionally efficient way for investors to own a portfolio of professionally managed securities.

CHAPTER 2

How To Read the Mutual Fund Listings

Many people who have owned mutual funds for years remain unclear about how to read the mutual fund listings in their daily newspapers. The information provided in these tables is important for both existing shareowners and potential investors. All of the major mutual funds can be found in the daily listings. From the information they provide, you can determine the following:

1. The individual mutual funds offered by each fund group
2. The price per share to purchase any mutual fund
3. The *net asset value* (NAV) or amount you will receive per share if a fund was sold on the trade date of the listing (less any applicable redemption charges or fees)
4. Which funds are "no-load," meaning those that charge no commission when you buy shares
5. The actual amount of the sales commission charged to purchase shares of "load" funds
6. Which funds have a redemption fee or contingent sales charge when shares are redeemed
7. Which funds use shareowners' assets to pay for distribution costs
8. Whether you will participate in the next income dividend or capital gains distribution
9. Which funds are about to pay a stock dividend or if the shares are to be split
10. The amount of any increase or decrease in the share price of each fund as compared to the previous trading day

This chapter explains what is meant by each entry in the printed tables. Figure 2.1 is an excerpt from the mutual fund tables published by the *New York Times* on March 3, 1992.

MUTUAL FUND GROUPS

On the left side of each column in Figure 2.1, the names of the mutual fund groups appear in bold letters and are often in abbreviated form. Directly under the group name are all the individual funds sold by that group. Some small or new funds may be omitted from the list if they have not attained certain requirements as to size and number of shareholders. Individual mutual funds that are not part of a group are printed in standard type.

At the top of the first column, note that "Price Funds" (for T. Rowe Price Funds) appears with its individual funds listed underneath. Each

FIGURE 2.1   Sample Mutual Fund Table

fund is abbreviated. For example, CalTF stands for the T. Rowe Price California Tax-Free Bond Fund, CapAp refers to the T. Rowe Price Capital Appreciation Fund and so on.

NAV AND BUY

Following each listed fund are the share prices that each fund closed at on the previous business day. The first figure is the NAV. For example, 11.26 indicates, in dollars and cents, the amount per share that an investor in the T. Rowe Price Capital Appreciation Fund would have received if the investor had sold his or her shares on that trade date. NAV represents the value of the total net assets of the fund divided by the total number of shares outstanding.

As you move across the table, the next item is the *buy* price, the cost to an investor who is buying shares. In the case of the T. Rowe Price Capital Appreciation Fund, NL is printed to indicate that it is a no-load fund. There is no commission or sales charge for funds sold by the T. Rowe Price Group, so the buy price would be the same as the NAV.

Looking across to the Templeton Group (two columns over), note that the buy price of each fund (except for the first) is higher than the NAV price. The difference between the two prices represents the sales charge, or *load*. The Templeton Group sells load funds, so the sales charge is added to the NAV per share, resulting in the buy or offer price of each share.

Just to the right of the buy price (or NL in the case of no-load funds) is an indication of any change in share prices from the next previous trading day. In the case of the T. Rowe Price Capital Appreciation Fund, the share price decreased by $.02 per share.

NOTATIONS

Because of the complexity of mutual fund commissions, fees and dividends, a system of notations and footnotes is used by the Associated Press. You will see some but not all of the notations in our excerpt from the published table. By referring to the footnotes (usually included with the mutual fund listings), it is possible to learn a good deal of important

FIGURE 2.2   Notations for the Sample Mutual Fund Table

e	Ex capital gains distribution. The person who buys this fund is not entitled to the next capital gains payout. The fund is being sold ex or without the distribution. When the fund went ex, the price per share dropped by the amount of the distribution, so there is no loss to an investor who purchases the shares now. (See Chapter 19—Timing Your Purchases To Avoid Taxes.)
s	Stock dividend or stock split has been declared.
x	Ex cash dividend. The shares are being sold ex or without the dividend. An investor who buys shares of this fund is not entitled to the next dividend payout. The share price dropped by the amount of the dividend on the day the shares went ex. (See Chapter 19.)
f	Previous day's quotation.
NL	The fund has no front-end load or sales charge.
p	Fund assets are used to pay for distribution costs (12b-1 plan).
r	A redemption fee or contingent sales charge may apply at the time shares are redeemed.
t	Both **p** and **r** apply.

Source: The Associated Press.

information about each of the funds you have an interest in. (See Figure 2.2.)

SUMMARY

The mutual fund listings found in the financial section of daily newspapers provide important information for both existing shareowners and potential investors. They normally include all the major mutual funds and enable you to determine the individual funds offered by each fund group, NAVs, whether funds are sold with or without sales charges and other helpful data.

CHAPTER 3

Why Big Investors Buy Mutual Funds

More and more substantial investors are using mutual funds to solve at least some of their investment problems. This trend accelerated with the development of money market funds in the 1970s. It is no longer unusual for large investors to place in excess of $1 million in mutual fund accounts.

Who are these investors and why do they do it? Many of them certainly can afford to hire their own investment managers on a private basis. Large shareholders of mutual funds today include wealthy individuals, trustees, pension and profit-sharing retirement plans, corporate funds, endowment funds and institutions such as churches, schools and hospitals. In the last analysis, big investors buy mutual funds for many of the same reasons as do small investors.

PERFORMANCE AND POLICY

One of the most important reasons why major investors choose mutual funds is the availability of past performance records. No other investment management form can provide prospective clients with so complete and unquestionable a picture of what it has achieved in the past. The investor can easily see how well any mutual fund manager has handled the funds under his or her care and if those results are suitable to the investor's own investment needs.

Of value, in addition to an accurate picture of past performance, is a mutual fund's clearly stated position relating to objectives, policies and investment holdings. Not only do mutual fund companies have a wide variety of different objectives and policies, they also provide clear descriptions of exactly what these objectives and policies are and how management goes about implementing them.

CONVENIENCE, SIMPLICITY AND LIQUIDITY

For all large investors, the convenience of owning shares in one or a few mutual funds is an important benefit. Contrast this with owning individual shares of stock in many companies, collecting dividends on each and having to keep records of each transaction. Record keeping alone is an important problem that is kept to a minimum by owning mutual funds.

Complete liquidity is another benefit that the large investor appreciates. A portion, or the entire amount, of a mutual fund investment can be liquidated quickly and without any concern about disrupting the market in a particular stock or bond.

Finally, with no-load mutual funds, an investor can get his or her money into and out of the market *at no cost*. There is no commission to buy and no cost to sell (in most cases), and no period of time that the investment must remain in effect. The investor has nearly complete flexibility in the handling of his or her money. Contrast this with the ownership of individual securities, where an investor must pay a commission to buy and again a commission to sell.

FREEDOM FROM CARE AND RESPONSIBILITY

Even experienced investors often reach the point where they no longer want the responsibility of managing their own investments. The financial universe has become so large and so complex that it is now virtually impossible for any individual to be competent in all its phases. Other investors simply want the peace of mind that comes from letting someone else do the worrying—managers get paid for it. Many investors have bought a stock that looked attractive, only to watch it immediately drop five or ten points in price. The volatility of such a stock in a mutual fund would hardly be noticed and is probably offset by another stock that is rising.

This brings us to *diversification*. Large and experienced investors have come to understand and appreciate the benefits of being diversified. Not only can an investor enjoy the advantages of diversification provided by one mutual fund, he or she also can further diversify by spreading assets over several different funds. This provides the additional safety of multiple managers, each of whom is governed by his or her own set of investment objectives and policies. Different managers, objectives and policies provide varying results in different economic and market climates, further reducing the risks in a large (or small) account.

TRUST ACCOUNTS

Mutual fund shares have become increasingly accepted as a prudent investment for trust accounts and by the banks and trust companies that manage them. This has been especially true with the advent of money market funds and with the growing acceptance of common stocks as suitable investments for trusts.

The *prudent man rule* is one that can easily be met by careful selection and investment in mutual funds. This standard was set forth in 1830 by Justice Samuel Putnam in the famous case of Harvard College v. Amory. As Justice Putnam stated: "All that can be required of a trustee . . . is that he shall conduct himself faithfully and exercise a sound discretion. He is to observe how men of prudence, discretion and intelligence manage their own affairs, not in regard to speculation, but in regard to the permanent disposition of their funds, considering the probable income as well as the probable safety of the capital to be invested . . . ."

The purchase of mutual fund shares answers the need for careful selection, adequate diversification and watchfulness that are essential to prudent investing in stocks and bonds. It is a job that requires continuous diligence. Many trustees, small institutions and individuals alike, simply do not have the time, background or expertise to undertake this effort. Beyond that, many small trusts do not have sufficient assets to provide the diversification required by prudence.

RETIREMENT PLANS AND INSTITUTIONS

For pension and profit-sharing plans, mutual funds offer various advantages. The fiduciary responsibilities implicit in these plans are similar to those faced by the trustees of personal trusts. By using mutual funds, corporate officers maintain control of the plans while meeting the fiduciary requirements of trustees. They can obtain the particular investment objectives and policies that are suitable for their plans while meeting Internal Revenue Service requirements for maintaining the plans' tax-exempt status.

A further advantage to retirement plans is the ease with which mutual fund investments can be evaluated for performance on an annual, or more frequent, basis. This can be difficult to accomplish for a plan that is invested in a variety of individual stocks and bonds. It is also simple to determine the value of a withdrawing participant's account and to reallocate any forfeited amounts among remaining participants.

Further simplifying the problems of setting up retirement plans is the availability of prototype pension and profit-sharing plans that have been developed by many mutual fund organizations. This makes it unnecessary for companies to go to the time and expense of having their own individual plans drawn up. *Individual retirement accounts* (IRAs) and retirement plans for self-employed individuals are also offered by many mutual fund groups.

Among the largest investors in the shares of mutual funds are schools, colleges, foundations, hospitals, church organizations, libraries, unions and fraternal associations. Such institutions do not have qualified personnel to handle the proper investment of their funds. But even when they do, they often find it more convenient and prudent to utilize mutual funds for the same reasons that other large investors find advantageous —namely, diversification, investment management and defined investment objectives and policies.

SUMMARY

Large investors utilize mutual funds for many of the same reasons as do smaller investors. By experience, they have found that mutual funds provide the benefits they seek in a more cost-effective and convenient way than would otherwise be possible. Some of the reasons to utilize mutual funds are as follows:

- Past performance is easily evaluated.
- Investment objectives and policies are clearly spelled out.
- A portfolio of investments can be set up quickly and at no cost.
- Accounts can be readily liquidated without disrupting the market.
- Investors are relieved of the responsibility and care of managing their investments.

CHAPTER 4

What Mutual Funds Will Do for You

Everyone who invests money does so for the purpose of realizing a return on his or her investment. The investor may want to obtain simple interest at the going rate, while at the same time being assured that there will be little or no risk to principal, as with a bank savings account, certificate of deposit or money market fund. Or the investor may want a higher rate of interest with a guarantee of the return of principal at a specified future time. This is possible with a U.S. government bond. However, market fluctuations in the value of bonds, which result from interest rate changes, might make the investment worth more or less than the investor paid for it if he or she must sell prior to the date it matures.

Another investor may seek growth through capital appreciation. He or she may not be so concerned about receiving current income and may be willing to assume a certain amount of risk from changes in the market valuation of the investment over time. But in the long run, such an investor anticipates a profit by being able to sell out for a higher price than he or she paid. In this case, an investment in common stocks would likely be the answer.

Many types of financial instruments are available to the person who wants to employ his or her capital productively. But achieving financial objectives is not always an easy task for an individual to accomplish alone, especially if the person is one of modest means. The reason lies in the difficulty and cost of obtaining three basics of prudent investing:

(1) careful selection of securities, (2) diversification and (3) liquidity. The beauty of mutual funds is that they provide the investor with all three.

PROFESSIONAL ADVICE

Some of the best and most highly compensated investment managers in the world are employed by mutual funds. Not only must they produce good returns on the assets committed into their care, but the performance of the funds they manage is continuously compared to various market indices, as well as to other mutual funds.

The mutual fund industry is highly competitive. Like the top-paid performers on professional sports teams, the mutual fund industry also has its superstars. They too are awarded very large compensation packages. The top managers become celebrities and are feted and sought after by television network talk shows. Some have fleeting fame after showing excellent results for a short time and then fall into obscurity when their funds suddenly lag behind, or worse, turn in substantial losses. Others who consistently deliver good performance over long periods of time see their funds continue to grow by attracting large numbers of new investors. The best mutual funds do whatever is necessary in an attempt to retain their top investment managers. With as little as $250 invested, the smallest mutual fund shareowner benefits from the same top-quality investment management as does the endowment fund that has invested $10 million or more.

DIVERSIFICATION

An important consideration in developing your investment program is to reduce risk as much as possible. Assets should be diversified among different types of investments, and also adequately diversified within each type. It's the old story of not putting all your eggs in one basket.

As will be discussed more fully in Chapter 5, the multitude of mutual fund companies makes available to the individual investor an enormous range of diversity. For example, by investing in mutual funds, a person with $10,000 can allocate $2,000 to U.S. government bonds, $2,000 to high-yielding corporate bonds, $2,000 to blue chip common stocks, $2,000 to the stocks of small emerging-growth companies and $2,000 to the stocks of other companies located all over the world! And the investor knows that through these funds he or she has an indirect interest in literally hundreds of different companies.

LIQUIDITY

Usually when people consider various investment alternatives, one of the first questions that comes to mind is "How quickly can I get to my money if I need it?" The ability readily to convert an asset to cash is called *liquidity,* an important characteristic for an investment to have.

The owner of mutual fund shares can convert his or her investment into cash quickly, conveniently and at an easily calculated value. In some cases, the owner can simply write a check for the amount of money needed. With other funds, the person can call the fund and ask for a redemption of the amount he or she wishes, and a check will be mailed within days. For faster action, the proceeds of redeemed shares can also be wired by the fund directly into the investor's own bank account. The share value of every fund is calculated at the end of each business day, so the investor can always keep abreast of what his or her shares are worth.

SPECIAL SERVICES THE FUNDS OFFER

With over 3,000 mutual funds in operation, the competition for your investment dollars is fierce. One of the ways funds woo your business is to offer a number of important and useful services. These services can help enormously in making your investing activities more profitable and convenient.

Account Statements

The service you will probably see and use most often is the *account statement.* It provides a complete record of your investment activity in the mutual fund and is essential for the preparation of future income tax returns. You will receive a statement pertaining to each mutual fund you own at least once a year, and more often if there is any activity in your account. A statement is generated whenever there is a purchase of additional shares, when shares are redeemed or if there is an administrative change (name and address, distribution option, etc.). Some funds also send a statement with every cash distribution they mail.

Accumulation Plan

The *accumulation plan* is perhaps the most popular service offered by mutual funds. Nearly all funds provide an arrangement whereby an investor can conveniently make additional investments to an account after an initial purchase of shares. Such investments can be made on a regular or irregular basis.

This informal type of program has facilitated investing for many purposes. It has attracted companies that invest substantial amounts for their pension and profit-sharing plans, as well as millions of individuals who invest money for their retirement, their children's education and so on. The accumulation plan lasts for just as long as the investor chooses to make additional purchases.

Bank draft investing recently has been made available by many mutual funds. On this basis, investments of a predetermined cash amount are made monthly or quarterly directly from a shareholder's checking account via bank drafts. In addition, an increasing number of mutual funds allow organized groups, as well as individuals, to set up accumulation plans through the use of a salary deduction or other group method of payment.

Reinvestment Privilege

One of the most useful and financially effective services mutual funds offer is to permit investors automatically to reinvest their income dividends and capital gains distributions into additional shares of the fund. Many investors who own individual issues of stocks and bonds have found that it is difficult to invest the dividend and interest payments they receive efficiently. The amounts are generally small and arrive intermittently. That problem is solved with mutual funds.

Most funds reinvest distributions into additional shares at NAV, although some charge a sales fee, reinvesting at the offering price. (The latter, of course, would never be the case with no-load funds.) A special service provided by some funds permits the reinvestment of one fund's dividends into shares of another fund in the same group.

The ability to compound share ownership through automatic reinvestment of dividends is the most certain of all methods of making an investment account grow.

Exchange Privilege

Under this arrangement, the shareowner has the right to exchange the shares owned in one fund for the shares of another fund that is part of the same group, or "family." There are many families of funds. Some of the largest groups will have as many as 60 or more funds. An exchange can be made for a nominal charge (usually five dollars) or in some cases for no charge at all.

While a mutual fund is meant to be a long-term investment, there are occasions when you might want to change from one type of fund to another. For example, you may want to further diversify your funds. Or, you may decide the time has come to move out of stocks and into bonds or into a money market fund, and so on. The point is that the exchange privilege adds an important degree of flexibility and control that the investor has over his money.

It is important to consider possible tax consequences before making an exchange. The exchange of shares in one fund for shares in another is considered a sale and new purchase for tax purposes. If at the time of transfer, the value of the shares being liquidated is greater than their original purchase cost, a capital gain is realized.

Automatic Withdrawal Plan

Most mutual funds permit investors to receive monthly (or less frequent) checks of a specified amount that are drawn against their fund accounts. Different funds will have various limitations on the use of this plan. In many cases, the funds require a minimum balance of $10,000 in the account. Also, there usually is a requirement that the withdrawal amount not exceed a stated percentage of the market value of the account or not be less than a certain dollar amount, such as $50.

Funds generally require that when a withdrawal plan is in effect, all income and capital gains distributions must be invested in additional shares. The amounts withdrawn under the automatic withdrawal plan may be more or less than the fund's income dividend amount. If it is more, the difference will have to come out of capital, creating the potential for the gradual erosion of an investor's principal.

Since a withdrawal plan is voluntary and flexible, it can be changed or terminated at any time by the shareowner. He or she retains complete control over the account.

Retirement Plans

Another important service that mutual funds provide to their share-holders is to make available convenient vehicles for investing in different types of tax-favored retirement plans.

Prototype Corporate Retirement Plans.   These plans can be adopted with a minimum of cost and red tape. The model prototype plans have been preapproved as to form by the Internal Revenue Service and are easily understood and set up. They are available for both pension and profit-sharing plans.

Individual Retirement Accounts (IRAs).   Created by the Employee Retirement Income Security Act of 1974, these plans allow certain individuals to set up tax-sheltered retirement plans of their own. Partici-pants can make annual contributions and also roll over lump-sum distri-butions from corporate pension and profit-sharing plans into their IRAs.

Simplified Employee Pension Plans (SEP).   These plans were designed primarily for businesses that do not have employee retirement plans and also may be used by those companies that do have plans, but with some limitations.

Keogh Custodial Accounts.   Many mutual funds provide this ser-vice for self-employed individuals who wish to have tax-sheltered retire-ment plans. These individuals may invest in mutual fund accounts and need only have an established plan and a bank custodial account.

Part Three of this book, "Tax-Advantaged Retirement Plans for Your Business," provides detailed information on such plans and how they can be used with mutual funds.

SUMMARY

There is no way other than by investing in mutual funds that an investor with limited resources can hope to obtain all the benefits of professional management, diversification, liquidity, administration and reporting. And these benefits can be had at minimal cost. The development of mutual funds has indeed been a miracle of capitalism.

CHAPTER 5

The Wide World of Mutual Funds

By early 1992 there were over 3,000 mutual funds being actively sold in the United States, with wide variances in size, age, purpose and policy. The oldest have been in existence for over 60 years; many have been established within the last 10 years. Some have only several million dollars under management, while others measure their assets in the billions. Obviously, no one fund can serve all investment purposes. The wide appeal of mutual funds depends in large part on the extensive diversity of types that are available.

One investor may seek the greatest potential for capital appreciation. Another may want a high level of current income, or to find a way to reduce income taxes. Others seek to offset the effects of inflation by maintaining the purchasing power of their assets or developing an income that will gradually increase over the years. With all this, most investors also are intensely interested in avoiding the loss of capital.

Each mutual fund is established with clearly stated investment objectives and management policies. These are set forth in the prospectus, which every investor must be given before purchasing shares in a fund. For example, the prospectus of one large money market fund states that its investment objective is to provide as high a level of current income as is consistent with the preservation of capital and the maintenance of liquidity. To achieve this goal, it describes the types of securities in which it will invest, states that it may seek to enhance yield through lending and borrowing practices and indicates that it may operate in the futures markets.

The investor should recognize that, to achieve a particular objective, a fund manager may have to engage in certain investment practices that involve an increased amount of risk and can result in an impairment of capital under adverse market conditions. The prospectus will spell out the types of risk that are present in connection with the stated investment policies.

TYPES OF MUTUAL FUNDS

The evaluation of standard investment objectives for the purpose of grouping mutual funds into categories is a matter of judgment based on the information provided in the policy statement found in each fund's prospectus. Commonly used investment objective classifications are listed below.

- *Adjustable-rate preferred fund*—Invests primarily in adjustable-rate preferred stock.
- *Balanced fund*—Its primary objective is to conserve principal by maintaining at all times a balanced portfolio of both stocks and bonds. The stock/bond ratio will typically range around 60 percent/40 percent.
- *Capital appreciation fund*—Aims at maximum capital appreciation, often by using leverage, heavy portfolio turnover, unregistered securities, options, etc. It may at times hold large cash positions.
- *Convertible securities fund*—Invests its portfolio primarily in convertible bonds and convertible preferred stocks.
- *Corporate bond fund*—Invests primarily in corporate bonds. The fund may also hold government bonds.
- *Equity income fund*—Looks for relatively high current income and growth of income by investing in equities offering these characteristics.
- *Flexible income fund*—Emphasizes generation of income by investing in bonds; preferred, convertible and/or common stocks; and warrants.
- *Global fund*—Invests at least 25 percent of its securities in securities traded outside the United States. It also may own U.S. securities.

- *GNMA fund*—Invests primarily in Government National Mortgage Association (GNMA) securities.
- *Growth and income fund*—Invests in companies expected to enjoy long-term earnings growth and that also pass along some of these earnings in dividend increases.
- *Growth fund*—Invests in companies whose long-term earnings are expected to grow faster than the stocks making up the major market indexes.
- *Health/biotechnology fund*—Invests primarily in companies engaged in health care, medicine and biotechnology.
- *High-current-yield fund*—Seeks high current yield from fixed-income securities. Tends to invest in lower-quality bonds.
- *Income fund*—Seeks high current income by investing primarily in bonds and preferred stocks.
- *International fund*—Invests in securities that trade primarily outside the United States.
- *Municipal bond fund*—Invests in the tax-exempt obligations of states, their agencies and municipalities.
- *Option growth fund*—Seeks to increase its net asset value (NAV) by investing a portion of its portfolio in options.
- *Option income fund*—Writes covered options on a substantial portion of its portfolio to increase income.
- *Precious metals fund*—Invests primarily in the shares of companies engaged in mining, processing or owning gold, silver and other precious metals.
- *Preferred stock fund*—Invests primarily in shares of preferred stock.
- *Science and technology fund*—Invests primarily in the shares of science and technology stocks.
- *Small-company growth fund*—Limits its investments to shares of stock in companies based on size, as described in the prospectus.
- *Specialty fund*—Invests in the shares of companies in a specific industry, such as banks, computers and health care; or it invests in a geographical area, such as the Sun Belt, Europe or the Pacific Basin.
- *U.S. government fund*—Invests in the securities issued by the U.S. government and its agencies.
- *Utility fund*—Invests primarily in shares of stock issued by public utility companies.

This listing, which is by no means all-inclusive, gives an idea of the types of groupings an investor may see when he or she looks at reference material or in popular financial magazines such as *Barron's, Business Week, Forbes* and *Money.*

SUMMARY

In this book we will take a somewhat different approach, looking at mutual fund investing from the point of view of the investor in terms of what he or she wants to accomplish. For example, is the investor looking for maximum capital growth, a consistent monthly income, preservation of capital with a competitive rate of return or some other specific objective?

What you want as an individual will depend on your own unique situation. The variables that lead you to determine your particular investment objectives will include such factors as your age, earning power, current assets, debts, family responsibilities, other obligations, risk tolerance and so on. This book is designed to help you develop an intelligent and consistent investment program and having done that, to accomplish your long-term financial aspirations.

CHAPTER 6

How the Funds Get Paid

All mutual fund companies are in business to make a profit. Many started out as investment managers for clients such as pension funds, college endowments, charitable trusts and wealthy private individuals. They charged fees ranging from as little as 0.5 percent to as much as 2 percent or more of the assets under their management. Over the years, the minimum amount of money investment managers would agree to manage has increased significantly. Today, few managers will handle as little as $100,000, and for many investment managers the minimum is much higher. Some managers will accept no less than $1 million, $5 million or even $10 million from a single client.

MUTUAL FUNDS ATTRACT ASSETS

There is a constant need to increase the cost-effectiveness of high-priced investment management talent. This has resulted in a proliferation of new mutual funds as a way to bring vast sums of money under management. The manager of a fund has in effect one client with one investment objective and a single set of investment policies. The larger the fund, the more cost-effective it becomes. While big funds require more personnel to run them than do small funds, the number of people needed becomes proportionately much smaller as the size of the fund grows.

However, we're not talking about small potatoes in terms of the size of costs and management fees. For example, the Fidelity Magellan

Fund, by far the largest of the growth funds, had $19.8 billion under management in early 1992. Expenses charged to the fund (including the management fee) amounted to approximately 1.06 percent of total net assets. This translated into more than $209 million in annual revenues to the Fidelity Group from this one fund. This fund carries a 3 percent sales charge.

Why is the Magellan Fund so big (the next largest growth fund had a little over $9 billion in assets)? The answer is performance. The Magellan Fund, begun in 1962, has had an outstanding record of investment performance. Money tends to move into those funds that investors believe will provide them with the highest return, consistent with their investment objectives and risk tolerance.

The expense charges of Magellan (at 1.06 percent of average net assets) are moderately low in the universe of some 3,000 mutual funds. The ratio of expenses to average net assets of growth funds range from as low as 0.35 percent for the Wellington Fund (more than $3 billion of assets) to as much as 2.92 percent for the Keystone International Fund ($73 million).

Expense charges will depend to some extent on the size and type of the fund. For example, a young and specialized fund such as the Medical Research Investment Company (begun in 1985) reported an expense ratio in 1987 of 6.08 percent on $2.9 million of average net assets invested. A fund's *expense ratio* is the proportion that expenses (costs of operation plus management fee) bears to net assets. This no doubt was a temporary aberration due to Medical Research Investment Company's small size. As the size of a fund increases, its expenses as a percent of its assets should drop dramatically. Funds that specialize in a particular investment area, such as medical research, will also frequently have higher costs than will those of general growth funds.

At the low end of the spectrum, as far as operating expenses are concerned, are six Vanguard Group municipal bond funds. They reported an expense ratio of only 0.25 percent of average net assets in 1991. The six funds ranged in size from $523 million to more than $2 billion in assets. All funds in the Vanguard family tend to have lower-than-average costs, but one reason for the low costs associated with municipal bond funds is the relative ease in managing them. There generally is little turnover of securities in the portfolio, and interest payments are collected by the fund only semiannually for each bond.

CHECK EXPENSES BEFORE YOU INVEST

Every mutual fund must report its expense charges annually in its prospectus. This makes it very easy for the investor to compare charges from one fund to another. Of course, expense charges are just one factor to consider in the selection of a fund. But again, other things being equal (management ability, past performance, investment objectives and policies), a fund with low expenses will tend to produce a better return for the investor than will one with charges that are out of line with the competition. Looking back on the past performance of mutual funds, this principle has generally been found to be true.

The management fee usually is the largest part of total expenses. It covers the salaries of fund officers and other employees as well as expenses relating to office space and facilities, and the payment for investment management and advice. Other operating expenses borne by a fund include charges of the fund's custodian, accountants and attorneys; the cost of issuing share certificates and disbursing dividends; and expenses for printing, postage and mailing.

Many funds have also put into effect a distribution services agreement (Rule 12b-1) adopted by the Securities and Exchange Commission (SEC) under the Investment Company Act of 1940. This permits mutual funds to directly or indirectly pay expenses connected with the distribution and marketing of its shares. These *12b-1 fees* range anywhere from 0.05 percent in some funds to as much as 1.25 percent in other funds. Such fees can have a very adverse impact on a fund's performance, especially as compared with similar funds that do not charge 12b-1 fees. The mutual fund listings in major daily newspapers will indicate which funds charge 12b-1 fees. (See Chapter 2, "How To Read the Mutual Fund Listings.")

Expenses are paid by a fund first out of investment income, which is more than sufficient in most cases. An exception would be for funds that invest entirely in growth companies that pay little or no dividends. Then expenses must come out of invested capital.

EXPENSES AS LISTED IN A PROSPECTUS

A good example of a fund that has kept its expenses to a minimum is the Windsor II fund, a no-load fund and member of the Vanguard Group. The information in Figure 6.1 appeared in its 1992 prospectus.

The no-load Vanguard Windsor Fund (not Windsor II) had net assets of more than $7.8 billion on September 30, 1991. Begun in 1958, the fund was so successful and grew so rapidly that for a time it has stopped accepting new accounts. Management has been concerned that the heavy influx of new money coming into the fund could negatively affect the fund's future performance. Windsor II, founded in 1985, does accept new investors.

FUNDS OCCASIONALLY CHARGE NO EXPENSES

Cutthroat competition in the mutual fund industry can make it very difficult for a new fund to build size quickly. This is especially true of money market funds, where yield differences are measured in basis points (a basis point is one 1/100 of 1 percent). In early 1989, the Dreyfus and Fidelity groups decided to bring out new money market funds that would invest not only in domestic but also in foreign money market instruments. Because of higher yields available abroad, these

FIGURE 6.1 Sample Expenses from Vanguard Windsor II Fund Prospectus

Shareholder Transaction Expenses

Sales load imposed on purchase	None
Sales load imposed on reinvested dividends	None
Redemption fees	None
Exchange fees	None

Annual Fund Operating Expenses

Management expenses	0.11%
Investment advisory fees	0.16
Shareholder accounting costs	0.16
12b-1 fees	None
Distribution costs	0.02
Other expenses	0.03
Total operating expenses	0.48%

Source: Reprinted by permission of The Vanguard Group.

funds would pay 20 to 40 basis points more interest than could funds that invest entirely in domestic "paper." But how could they get off the ground and into the big time quickly?

The answer was to waive all expense charges initially, with the fund companies absorbing those charges themselves. By doing this, the funds added 60 to 70 basis points to the yield. This, together with the extra interest from foreign securities, enabled them to offer yields a full 1 percent above what the competition was paying. Both companies began an intensive national advertising blitz. On April 23, 1990, Fidelity's Spartan Money Market Fund announced that they had gone from zero to $1 billion in assets in three months! This was an unprecedented achievement. By the end of 1990, the Fidelity Spartan Money Market Fund was managing more than $7 billion, and the Dreyfus Worldwide Dollar Money Market Fund held more than $9.5 billion in assets.

For the investor, this was a time to take advantage of a short-term gift. These extra high rates, made possible by the waiving of expenses, would last only until the fund managers decided to start cashing in themselves by applying their normal charges. When they did that, the yields investors received would drop by the amount of the expense ratio. In the meantime, investors in these funds were earning 10.7 percent, while competing funds were paying about 9.8 percent.

For Fidelity, which has an expense ratio of approximately 0.42 percent on its other money market funds, income from the new fund (at the $7.5 billion level) would run in the neighborhood of $31.5 million a year. Not bad for a new product after two years.

SUMMARY

As we stated in the Introduction, nothing is free. The price is time, effort or money. Mutual funds provide a cost-effective solution for the individual or organization seeking professional managements of funds. With little effort, the investor can determine which funds charge reasonable management fees and keep operating expenses to a minimum; and he or she can avoid all sales charges by investing in true no-load funds.

CHAPTER 7

How a Prospectus Can Help You

Perhaps the most important source of information afforded mutual fund investors is the *prospectus.* The law stipulates that the offering of any mutual fund for sale to the public must be accompanied or preceded by a prospectus.

A prospectus sets forth concisely the information that a prospective investor should know about a specific mutual fund before investing. For more detailed information, a *statement of additional information* may be obtained without charge by writing or calling the mutual fund company. (Use their toll-free line.) The statement, which is incorporated by reference into the prospectus, has been filed with the Securities and Exchange Commission (SEC). Each prospectus also is required to display prominently the following words: "These securities have not been approved or disapproved by the Securities and Exchange Commission or any state securities commission nor has the Securities and Exchange Commission or any state securities commission passed upon the accuracy or adequacy of this prospectus. Any representation to the contrary is a criminal offense."

Before permitting a mutual fund company to offer a fund for sale to the public, the SEC examines the statement of additional information to be sure it contains all the information required by law. When that requirement has been met, the fund company is notified that it may offer its fund for sale to the public.

For illustration purposes, certain information contained in the March 1, 1992 prospectus of the Wellington Fund (a member of the Vanguard group of mutual funds) is set forth in the following paragraphs. This same type of data will be found in the prospectuses of most mutual funds.

WHAT THE PROSPECTUS CONTAINS

Investment Objectives and Policies

The first page of the 1992 prospectus of the Wellington Fund sets forth in typical fashion the information a typical investor wants to know about the investment objectives and policies of the fund. It states that the Wellington Fund "is a no-load, open-end diversified investment company designed to provide conservative investors with a prudent investment program." The *objectives* of the fund "include conservation of principal, a reasonable income return and profits without undue risk." There is no assurance that the fund will achieve its stated objectives.

The fund's *policy* is to invest "in a diversified portfolio of common stocks and bonds, with common stocks expected to represent 60 to 70 percent of the fund's total assets." A more detailed statement of the fund's investment policies is set forth later in the body of the prospectus. It explains how long securities are expected to be held, the percentage of securities to be held in fixed-income securities and the types and quality of those securities. It states that the fund may also invest in foreign securities, index futures and options, and preferred stocks. It further states that the investment objectives and policies may be changed by the board of directors but that shareholders are notified prior to any material change in either.

Fund Expenses

The prospectus of each fund includes a table that illustrates all the expenses and fees a shareholder of the fund incurs. Shareholder transaction expenses include a sales load imposed on purchases, a sales load imposed on reinvested dividends, redemption fees and exchange fees. In the case of most true no-load funds, there are no charges for any of these activities. Other funds will indicate their charges as a percentage of net asset value or dollar amount. See Figure 7.1 for an example of how the Wellington Fund prospectus sets forth its charges.

FIGURE 7.1   Sample Expenses from Wellington Fund Prospectus

Shareholder Transaction Expenses

Sales load imposed on purchases	None
Sales load imposed on reinvested dividends	None
Redemption fees	None
Exchange fees	None

Annual Fund Operating Expenses

Management expenses	0.09%
Investment advisory fees	0.07
Shareholder accounting costs	0.14
12b-1 fees	None
Distribution costs	0.02
Other expenses	0.03
Total operating expenses	0.35%

Source: Reprinted by permission of The Vanguard Group.

Selected Per-Share Data and Ratios

The Wellington Fund's 1992 prospectus provides a table with selected per-share data and ratios (shown for a share outstanding throughout each year) for the most recent ten-year period. This table is reproduced in Figure 7.2. It is part of the fund's financial statements and permits an investor to see how ably the fund was managed during the ten-year period ending November 30, 1991.

Investment Risks

Every prospectus points out that, like any investment program, a mutual fund entails certain risks. A fund investing in common stocks is subject to stock market risk—that is, the possibility that stock prices in general will decline over short or even extended periods. The stock market tends to be cyclical, with periods when stock prices generally rise or decline.

To illustrate the volatility of stock prices, Figure 7.3 sets forth the extremes for U.S. stock market returns as well as the average return for the period 1926–91, as measured by the Standard & Poor's 500 Composite Stock Price Index.

FIGURE 7.2   Selected Per Share Data and Ratios from Wellington Fund's 1992 Prospectus

	Year Ended November 30,									
	1982	1983	1984	1985	1986	1987	1988	1989	1990	1991
Net Asset Value, Beginning of Year	$10.04	$11.05	$12.49	$12.08	$13.99	$16.06	$14.92	$16.82	$18.40	$16.29
Investment Activities										
Income	.94	.99	1.00	.99	1.03	1.02	1.04	1.09	1.08	1.02
Expenses	(.07)	(.08)	(.07)	(.08)	(.09)	(.07)	(.08)	(.07)	(.07)	(.06)
Net Investment Income*	.87	.91	.93	.91	.94	.95	.96	1.02	1.01	.96
Net Realized and Unrealized Gains										
(Losses)	1.01	1.88	.06	2.22	2.41	(1.55)	2.06	2.12	(1.46)	1.71
Total from Investment Activities	1.88	2.79	.99	3.13	3.35	(.60)	3.02	3.14	(.45)	2.67
Distributions										
Net Investment Income	(.87)	(.91)	(.92)	(.92)	(.94)	(.54)	(.98)	(.98)	(1.06)	(1.01)
Realized Net Gains	—	(.44)	(.48)	(.30)	(.34)	—	(.14)	(.58)	(.60)	—
Total Distributions	(.87)	(1.35)	(1.40)	(1.22)	(1.28)	(.54)	(1.12)	(1.56)	(1.66)	(1.01)
Net Asset Value,										
End of Year	$11.05	$12.49	$12.08	$13.99	$16.06	$14.92	$16.82	$18.40	$16.29	$17.95
Ratio of Expenses to Average Net Assets	.69%	.64%	.59%	.64%	.53%	.43%	.47%	.42%	.43%	.35%
Ratio of Net Investment Income to Average										
Net Assets	8.59%	7.09%	7.52%	6.84%	5.88%	5.56%	5.88%	5.77%	5.99%	5.39%
Portfolio Turnover Rate	38%	30%	27%	27%	25%	27%	28%	30%	33%	35%
Shares Outstanding,										
End of Year (thousands)	50,226	49,422	50,016	55,631	68,624	85,362	90,816	110,568	142,224	193,479

FIGURE 7.3 Average Annual U.S. Stock Market Returns
(1926–91) over Various Time Horizons

	1 Year	5 Years	10 Years	20 Years
Best	+53.9%	+23.9%	+20.1%	+16.9%
Worst	−43.3	−12.5	− 0.9	+ 3.1
Average	+12.3	+10.0	+10.3	+10.4

Source: Reprinted by permission of The Vanguard Group.

Performance Record

Investment results for several periods throughout a fund's lifetime help an investor see how money invested in a fund has fared in the past. Figure 7.4 shows the Wellington Fund's total-return investment performance, which assumes the reinvestment of all capital gains and income dividends for the indicated periods. Also included is comparative information with respect to two performance indexes: (1) the Composite Index, a measure of the investment performance of a balanced portfolio of stocks and bonds comprised of the Standard & Poor's 500 Composite Stock Price Index (65 percent) and the Salomon Brothers High Grade Bond Index (35 percent) and (2) the Consumer Price Index, a statistical measure of changes in the prices of goods and services.

Opening an Account

Each prospectus includes information on how to open an account and purchase shares in the fund and will be accompanied by an *account registration form.* Your purchase must be equal to or greater than the minimum initial investment. For different funds, this may range anywhere from as little as $50 to as much as $50,000 or more. Most funds can be started in the $1,000 to $3,000 range.

Fund shares may be purchased by mail, by wire, by exchange from another fund in the same family of funds, directly from your checking account and by other means that will be explained in the prospectus. When opening a new account, you must select one of four distribution options:

1. *Automatic reinvestment option*—Both dividends and capital gains distributions will be reinvested in additional shares of the fund.

FIGURE 7.4   Average Annual Return for Wellington Fund

	Percentage Increase		
Fiscals Periods Ended 11/30/91	**Wellington Fund**	**Composite Index**	**Consumer Price Index**
1 year	+16.8%	+19.1%	+3.0%
5 years	+ 9.6	+11.3	+4.5
10 years	+15.0	+15.7	+3.9
Lifetime*	+ 7.7	+ 8.3	+3.4

*December 27, 1929 to November 30, 1991.

Source: Reprinted by permission of The Vanguard Group.

2. *Cash dividend option*—Your dividends will be paid in cash and capital gains will be reinvested in additional fund shares.
3. *All-cash option*—Dividend and capital gains distributions will be paid in cash.

Some funds permit distributions to be reinvested automatically in shares of another fund of the same family.

Important Tax Note:

Be aware that if you purchase shares shortly before a distribution of dividends or capital gains, a portion of your investment will be returned to you as a taxable distribution (regardless of whether you are reinvesting your distributions or taking them in cash). See Chapter 19, "Timing Your Purchases To Avoid Taxes."

Other Important Information

The prospectus contains other information that you will find helpful in establishing and maintaining a mutual fund investment.

- *Signature guarantees*—Most funds require that for certain written transaction requests, your signature must be guaranteed by a bank, trust company or member of a domestic stock exchange. Having a document notarized does not qualify as a signature guarantee.
- *Certificates*—Most funds will issue share certificates on request.

- *Canceling trades*—A trade received by a fund in writing or by telephone, if believed to be authentic, may not normally be canceled. This would include purchases, exchanges or redemptions.
- *Trade dates*—These are the dates on which accounts are credited. If a purchase or sale is received by 4:00 P.M. (eastern standard time), the trade date is the date of receipt. If received after 4:00 P.M., the trade date is the next business day.
- *Exchanges*—Shares can be sold by exchanging into another mutual fund in the same family of funds. It is important to remember that this constitutes a taxable event, and any gain or loss is reportable for income tax purposes. (Many funds charge a small fee— e.g., $5—for exchanges.)
- *Other services*—The prospectus explains special services and options that are available to the investor, such as automatic investment plans, automatic withdrawal plans, telephone services and so on.

SUMMARY

The prospectus is arguably the most important tool available to a prospective mutual fund investor. A well-written prospectus is easy to read and provides a wealth of essential information, including investment objectives and policies, expenses and fees, historical performance data, a guide on how to open an account and the various services furnished by the fund.

CHAPTER 8

Laws That Protect You

It has been said that "there is no legislation that can prevent a fool from being parted from his [or her] money." It is also true that there is no way to protect investors against the results of bad management. However, over the years important laws have been enacted to prevent many possible abuses of trust. These laws are clear-cut and far-reaching. In this chapter we will summarize the key laws that affect mutual funds.

SECURITIES ACT OF 1933

The Securities Act of 1933 is the most important of the laws governing the sale of mutual fund shares. Nearly all mutual fund companies of any size are subject to this act when they sell new shares to the public. The law basically requires that the fund company must furnish accurate and full information in connection with financial and other corporate matters, so that the investor has the necessary facts on which to base an intelligent judgment regarding the value of the securities being offered. This information must be filed by the fund company with the Securities and Exchange Commission (SEC) in the form of a *registration statement*. The SEC then will review it for accuracy and completeness, allowing shares of the fund to be sold to the public only after it is satisfied as to its truthfulness and that no important matters have been omitted.

The fact that the SEC permits shares of a fund to be sold does not in any way imply its approval of the fund, nor does it imply that the fund is a good investment. When the SEC permits a registration statement to become effective, it merely indicates that the fund has apparently disclosed all the information that the law requires. If it turns out that the fund has falsified information in the registration statement, even though the SEC did not discover it, the law provides that the injured shareowner may sue the responsible persons.

The items in a registration statement of most interest to investors must be furnished in the form of a prospectus to the purchaser of any new security. Although an oral offer to sell may be made without a prospectus, any written offer must be accompanied by a prospectus. The prospectus should always be read carefully before anyone invests in a mutual fund (or any other newly issued security).

SECURITIES EXCHANGE ACT OF 1934

The Securities Exchange Act of 1934 serves in various ways to protect investors in mutual fund shares. It enables the SEC to impose minimum financial and accounting standards on broker-dealers engaged in interstate commerce and subjects them to periodic inspections. In addition, this act requires the SEC to supervise the national stock exchanges to prevent unlawful manipulation of securities prices, which helps protect investors in closed-end investment funds. The act also makes it unlawful to purchase or sell securities by fraudulent means in interstate commerce.

INVESTMENT COMPANY ACT OF 1940

The Investment Company Act of 1940 is also administered by the SEC. It supplements the other state and federal laws and provides a comprehensive system of regulation for the protection of investors. This act was adopted after the SEC had made a thorough study of investment companies and their practices.

The law specifically avoids any attempt to interfere with the exercise of management's judgment in the selection of investments and in no way does it purport to guarantee an investor against loss. It is aimed at preventing certain abuses and eliminating conflicts of interest on the part of those involved in managing the business of an investment company.

The Investment Company Act of 1940 does intend to:

- Provide investors with complete and accurate information as to the nature of investment company securities and the policies, financial responsibility and circumstances of investment companies and their management.
- Ensure that investment companies are organized and operated for the benefit of all shareholders rather than for the benefit of officers, directors, investment advisors or other special interest groups.
- Prevent inequitable provisions in investment company securities and protect the preferences and privileges of outstanding securities.
- Prevent undue concentration of control through pyramiding and other devices, and discourage management by irresponsible persons.
- Ensure sound accounting methods.
- Require adequate assets or reserves for the conduct of business.
- Prevent major changes in organization or business without the consent of shareholders.

INVESTMENT COMPANY AMENDMENTS ACT OF 1970

The Investment Company Amendments Act of 1970 formalized the first major revision in 30 years of the Investment Company Act of 1940. The major changes established by this act included new standards for management fees and mutual fund sales charges.

It is now provided that the price at which mutual fund shares are sold to the public shall not include "an excessive sales load." Rules on how that is to be defined were assigned to the National Association of Securities Dealers. The top sales charge in the mutual fund industry today is ordinarily 8.5 percent of the total payment, or 9.3 percent of the amount invested.

STATE LAWS

Blue-sky laws enacted by the various states regulate the sale of securities, including mutual funds, within the individual states. They cannot be summarized briefly because of the wide variety of their provisions. A few states go so far as to regulate such matters as sales commissions and investment policies.

In addition, since mutual funds are incorporated under state general corporation law, they are regulated as to the mechanics by which a fund company conducts its business. These laws, which vary widely, are not designed necessarily to protect mutual fund shareholders. Nonetheless, they are an essential part of the total legal protection afforded security holders of mutual funds domiciled in the United States.

SUMMARY

Mutual funds are probably the most closely regulated sector of the entire securities industry. While there is no way to protect investors from losses due to poor management or market fluctuations, the laws governing mutual fund companies are far-reaching and clear-cut.

PART TWO

Using Mutual Funds

CHAPTER 9

How To Start an Investment Program

If we had no concern for our future needs and aspirations, we would have no reason to invest. A young man who recently won $23 million in the Florida lottery announced that he had worked his last day. Various family members were also told they could quit their jobs; he would take over their support. The state promised to pay him over a million dollars a year for the next 20 years. At the end of 20 years he said he would win another lottery.

Most of us recognize that we must plan for our financial future. There is the inevitable rainy day, the cost of our children's education, opportunities that may require funds, a time when our earned income will stop and a day when we might like to rest. There are all kinds of reasons why the prudent person accumulates and invests assets for future needs.

A most important step to take first is to set for ourselves clear and reasonable investment objectives. This is the starting point of any successful program of building assets. Strangely, it is a step that is often overlooked or simply given lip service.

Many times I have had people with money to invest call me and ask, "What looks good?" When I inquired as to what they wanted to accomplish, the response usually was voiced with some surprise, "to make money!" They wanted to hear about something that was paying an extra high yield or a stock that would double *soon*. Such investors are looking for a free lunch, but there aren't many. High-yielding bond funds carry a commensurately high risk. Volatile stocks can go up fast—and come down fast.

The successful investor knows exactly what he or she is looking for. Such an individual has previously made a thoughtful evaluation of his or her family situation, health, age, finances, career path, risk tolerance (i.e., how much risk he or she is comfortable with) and, perhaps, a dream that the individual hopes will be a part of his or her future. In addition, the investor has talked with knowledgeable people he or she trusts to gain insights into what works, how long it takes, what risks are involved and what results to expect over time.

SPREAD THE RISK BY DIVERSIFYING YOUR ASSETS

Nearly everyone is familiar with the old adage "Don't put all your eggs in one basket." Andrew Carnegie, the Scottish-born industrialist who built a great steel company a hundred years ago said, "Put all your eggs in one basket, and watch that basket!" In Carnegie's case, he was in charge of the basket, and he also was willing to accept huge risks.

However, most investors are not in charge of the basket; they put their money into baskets that other people control. Investors face all kinds of risk in buying publicly traded securities. Some risks are related to the industry, the economy, interest rates, inflation, labor problems, lawsuits, supply shortages, competition and government controls. There also are risks regarding management: Is it competent? Is it honest? What happens if the key person dies? Is the company run for the benefit of the stockholders or for its management? Will they preserve the integrity of the bond ratings, or will they let their investment-grade bonds fall to junk-bond status by issuing large amounts of new debt?

The prudent investor reduces risk through diversification. This is done in two basic ways: (1) by investing money in different types of financial instruments and (2) by diversifying within each type. A wide range of investment vehicles is available in the financial world. These vehicles range from the very safe to the wildly speculative. Here is a short list, beginning with the safest (1) and moving toward the speculative (10).

1. Federally insured certificates of deposit
2. Life insurance company guaranteed annuities
3. U.S. Treasury securities (subject to fluctuation in market value)
4. Money market funds
5. Investment-grade bonds

6. Lower-grade bonds
7. Preferred and common stocks
8. Real estate
9. Limited partnerships
10. Commodities

DEVELOP A PLAN

Mutual funds represent a way to participate in the various types of financial instruments included in the preceding list, depending on the securities they hold (government bonds, corporate or municipal bonds, stocks, etc.) and their management policies.

In allocating your assets among the various alternatives, consider your need for ready cash. It is often said that one should keep about six months of income in cash equivalents. A sudden illness, the loss of a job, an accident or some other unexpected need for cash might upset a long-term investment program that lacks sufficient cash reserves. Money market funds are an excellent vehicle for this purpose.

Next consider the portion of your funds that you want to feel absolutely comfortable with from a safety standpoint, and to which you won't need immediate access. These funds should earn a reasonable rate of return and should not be subject to market fluctuations. The percentage will vary considerably between investors, depending on their individual needs and personal perspectives. Insured certificates of deposit might provide a good choice for this purpose. Another possibility is the single payment annuity sold by insurance companies (which permits your interest to accumulate tax-deferred).

After constructing the safety-net part of your financial plan, you come to the point where mutual funds can play an important role. The two main objectives that mutual funds fulfill best are growth and income. We will consider in some detail later how to invest for growth (Chapter 11, "Investing for Growth") and how to invest for income (Chapter 12, "Investing for Income"). But at this point, think in terms of the balance you want between these two broad objectives and how much risk you are willing to take. Incidentally, mutual funds also provide what is arguably the best way to maintain cash reserves, through the use of money market funds.

The trustees responsible for the investment of large pools of money, such as pension and profit-sharing plans, set specific percentages of their funds to be in stocks, bonds and cash equivalents. These are matters of investment policy and are subject to change over time as economic or market conditions change. A typical allocation among these broad classes of assets might be 50 percent in stocks, 35 percent in bonds and 15 percent in cash reserves. For the prudent individual investor as well, it makes sense to plan your strategy, develop an investment formula you can follow and then stick with it.

SUMMARY

The need to plan for the future and build a financial base is apparent to most of us. In doing so, the first step is to develop a plan about how this will be accomplished. Be realistic about your goals. Set clear and achievable objectives you can live with. Consider your personal tolerance for risk and the types of financial instruments you feel comfortable with. Then consider what proportion of your funds to allocate to cash reserves, debt instruments and equities. Finally, success in investing requires perseverance. Take the long view. Be patient and give your funds time to work. In the long run, you will reap a bountiful harvest.

CHAPTER 10

Investing the Way the Pros Do

How would you like to walk into your local bank and be told there is a 4 percent sales charge to buy a certificate of deposit? Perhaps your reaction would be "Do you mean to tell me that I have to pay you 4 percent for the privilege of putting my money in your bank?" But the banker would say, "This is a good deal. The other banks in town are charging fees of up to 8.5 percent for the same thing." Banks don't do this (although they do charge stiff penalties for early withdrawals); but many mutual funds have been charging fees for years. Such a fee is called a *load*, and it's totally unnecessary for you to pay it.

The only reason for a mutual fund to levy a sales charge is to cover costs of distribution. Most of the charge (about 85 percent) goes to the broker-dealer that handles the sale. Of that amount, about one-third goes to the salesperson (registered representative) who handles the transaction for the customer. The other 15 percent stays with the mutual fund's own sales arm.

The pros don't play this game. They buy directly and pay no commissions to anyone. You should do the same, and this chapter will tell you how.

INVESTING WITHOUT A BROKER AND WITHOUT COMMISSIONS

One of the great opportunities available to the investor today is the ability to buy into diversified, professionally managed portfolios of stocks and bonds at no cost. This is easily done by investing in *no-load* mutual funds. These funds sell their shares directly to the public, and with no sales charge.

An increasing number of all mutual funds are no-load funds. Over 500 no-load funds are priced daily in the mutual funds section of the *New York Times*, *The Wall Street Journal* and other major newspapers. They can be purchased on a direct basis and at no cost to the investor. There are, of course, expenses and management fees that are common to both load and no-load funds. These charges, which are generally small, are discussed in Chapter 6, "How the Funds Get Paid."

Not all no-load funds are as widely known to the general investing public as the load funds, where a sales commission is involved. This is because many people get their information from stock brokers, who quite naturally are reluctant to provide information on mutual funds that pay no commission. However, brokers do serve an important function in giving investment information to those people who either can't or don't want to take the time to become informed directly on their own.

Now let's take a look at the two principal ways in which open-end mutual funds are marketed.

LOAD FUNDS

These are the mutual funds that are normally distributed through investment broker-dealers. Sales charges, which are described in their prospectuses, run anywhere up to 8.5 percent of the dollar amount paid for the mutual fund. The amount of the sales charge is divided, with a small portion usually going to the sales arm of the mutual fund and the main portion going to the broker-dealer. Of the amount going to the broker-dealer, the firm may get roughly 65 percent and the individual broker about 35 percent. Sales charges can be paid at the time of purchase (a *front-end load*) or when the shares are redeemed (a *back-end load*). In some cases there may be a small charge at the time of purchase (a *low-load*) and another charge at redemption.

Mutual fund shares with front-end loads are offered for sale at a price marked up from the *net asset value* or *NAV* (the value of all assets held in a fund divided by the total number of shares outstanding) by the amount of the sales charge. The result is called the *offering price*.

Newspapers that carry a daily listing of mutual funds usually list both the NAV and the offering price (including the maximum sales charge) for each fund. A person buying shares of a fund will pay the offering price; a person selling shares will receive the NAV.

The sales charge on a front-end load fund is usually tiered, with *break-points* at different dollar purchase amounts. Figure 10.1 is an example of a typical schedule of sales charges for purchasing shares of a front-end load fund, which you would find in its prospectus.

A fairly recent development in the marketing of mutual funds has been the back-end load. Under this arrangement, shares are purchased at the net NAV. The investor pays no sales charge at the time of purchase. However, the salesperson must be paid, so the investor will pay a deferred sales charge if he or she redeems the shares prior to the end of a stipulated holding period. The amount of the charge declines over time until it eventually disappears entirely. There are usually no break-points for large purchases in back-end load funds.

An investor in back-end load funds is subject to a sales charge if he or she redeems shares within the first six years after purchase. Typical charges range from 5 percent for shares redeemed in the first year to 0 percent after six years. Early withdrawal charges are assessed as follows:

Year after Purchase	Withdrawal Charge
First year	5%
Second year	4
Third year	3
Fourth year	2
Fifth year	2
Sixth year	1
After six years	0

It may seem that an investor who holds on to a back-end fund for more than the stipulated holding period avoids any sales cost, but this is not the case. The money to pay sales and other costs of distributing shares is charged against the fund's income in accordance with Rule 12b-1 under the Investment Company Act of 1940.

Rule 12b-1 fees are assessed by many mutual funds, but they are especially high in the case of back-end load funds because such funds must recoup the commissions paid to salespeople. The fee charged by back-end load funds is typically 1.25 percent each year.

FIGURE 10.1   Sample Schedule of Sales Charges

Amount of Purchase (in Thousands)	Sales Charge as a Percentage of	
	Offering Price	Net Asset Value
Less than $100	4.50%	4.71%
$100 to $250	3.50	3.61
$250 to $500	2.60	2.67
$500 to $1,000	2.00	2.04
$1,000 to $3,000	1.00	1.01
$3,000 to $5,000	0.50	0.50
$5,000 and over	0.25	0.25

The investor should carefully consider the effect a substantial annual 12b-1 fee will have on his investment return. In some back-end loaded mutual funds, the 12b-1 fee decreases after the end of the early withdrawal period, but in most cases the fee continues indefinitely. The 12b-1 fee can have a dramatic negative impact on a fund's long-term total return. For example, consider two funds that are each invested in a portfolio of corporate bonds with an average income yield of 9 percent. Both funds have an expense ratio of 1 percent, resulting in a net income of 8 percent. One fund pays out the full net income to its shareholders, providing them with a dividend distribution rate of 8 percent. The other fund, a back-end load fund with the same 1 percent expense ratio and charging an additional 1.25 percent annual 12b-1 fee, is able to provide its shareholders with a dividend distribution rate of only 6.75 percent.

NO-LOAD FUNDS

These funds do not impose any sales charges. Their shares can be bought directly from the fund without using a broker and without paying any commissions. All other things being equal (investment performance, operating expenses, various fees, investor services, etc.), you can save a great deal of money and increase your investment return significantly by investing in no-load funds.

The mutual fund listings in major daily newspapers often indicate the loads and sales charge policies that apply to different funds. For example, the *New York Times* identifies no-load funds by printing *NL* where the offer or buy price would normally be found. In addition, *p* tells the reader that fund assets are used to pay distribution costs (12b-1 plan), *r* indicates that a redemption fee or contingent deferred sales charge may apply and *t* means that both *p* and *r* apply.

In the so-called true no-load funds, none of these charges apply. If you are in any doubt about what charges may apply to the particular funds in which you have an interest, just call the funds. Nearly all funds have 800 numbers, and they will be happy to answer your questions and mail you a prospectus. Toll-free 800 numbers can be obtained at no charge by dialing 1-800-555-1212. Just ask the operator for the toll-free number of the fund group in which you are interested. The toll-free numbers of many of the larger no-load funds are listed in Appendix B ("Directory of No-Load Mutual Funds").

Since no-load mutual fund companies sell their shares directly to the public without the use of investment brokers, it is up to the investor to take the initiative by contacting the mutual fund.

Note:

At the time this book went to press, the Securities and Exchange Commission had just released a report proposing sweeping changes for the mutual funds industry. The commission's report comes after two years of study and is expected to deregulate fund sales charges (making fund sales commissions negotiable, which could make them lower) to make it easier for investors to shop for funds based on expenses and to limit the combined amount of sales commissions and 12b-1 fees that a fund can charge. If implemented, all of this will be welcome news for the mutual fund investor.

SUMMARY

The savvy mutual fund investor will deal directly with no-load funds without going through a broker or broker-dealer. Most fund companies have toll-free 800 numbers and encourage investors to contact them for information and free literature. It is easy to identify no-load funds in the mutual fund section of your daily newspaper. Each no-load fund will be designated by an *NL* or *n*. A listing of no-load funds with their toll-free numbers is included at the back of this book. Unless there is a particular fund that you simply must have, we recommend that you steer away from any funds that levy a sales charge, front-end or back-end.

CHAPTER 11

Investing for Growth

Mutual funds are designed for long-term investing. Most fund managers take the long view in developing and executing their investment strategies. The concept of investing for the long pull is nowhere more important than for the investor whose investment objective is growth of capital.

THE WINDSOR FUND

An illustration of the rewards of growth fund investing and the need for patience can be found in a hypothetical $10,000 investment made in the Windsor Fund at its inception 30 years ago. Organized in October 1958, Windsor is the largest fund in the Vanguard group of investment companies. Its primary objective is long-term growth of capital and income for its shareholders. A secondary objective is current income. Although the fund seeks to accomplish these objectives mainly through investment in equity securities, it may invest without restriction in high-grade bonds and preferred stocks. The fund puts emphasis on industries and companies believed to have particularly favorable long-term prospects for appreciation, based on increasing earnings and dividends.

The patient investor in the Windsor Fund has been amply rewarded. A hypothetical $10,000 investment made in October 1958 at the fund's inception (with all income distributions reinvested in additional shares) would have had a value of $523,366 on December 31, 1991, a period of 33 years. In contrast, a hypothetical investment of $10,000 made in October 1958 in the Standard & Poor's 500 Index (with dividends reinvested) would have been worth $287,968 on December 31, 1991. The net asset value (NAV) of one share in the Windsor Fund at its inception was $5.52 (adjusted for a 2-for-1 stock split on May 31, 1969). Its value on December 31, 1991, with all income dividends and capital gains having been reinvested, was $288.90.

Even with this outstanding example of successful long-term mutual fund investing, there were times along the way that would try an investor's patience. In 1962, after four years of positive returns, the Windsor Fund dropped 25 percent in value. In that same year, the S&P 500 Index lost only 8.7 percent. There have been other years when the Windsor Fund underperformed the averages, had annual returns of only 1 percent to 7.5 percent or showed losses.

Since 1988, when the Windsor Fund substantially outperformed the S&P 500 (+28.7 percent to +16.5 percent), it has underperformed the index in 1989, 1990 and 1991. But overall the fund has done very well, providing an exceptional return to the investor who has stayed with it through thick and thin. The average annual return over the life of the fund (from October 1958 through December 31, 1991), assuming reinvestment of dividend and capital gains distributions, was 12.7 percent. (See Figure 11.1.)

APPROACHES TO INVESTING FOR GROWTH

There are almost as many individual mutual fund approaches to investing for growth as there are investment managers trying to do it. Each manager tends to develop a personal style, based on his or her concept of how best to achieve the elusive goal of making capital grow. For convenience, a limited number of fund classifications are generally recognized, based on broad investment objectives and policies. In many cases a particular fund will not fit neatly into any one of these classifications, so analysts include it in the group they feel it most nearly matches.

Within these fund groupings there are wide individual differences between the funds as to their specific investment objectives and policies, as well as in their investment performance. It is useful, though, to compare the average performance of funds over a period of time within each of the various categories.

FIGURE 11.1   Windsor Fund Total Investment Return

Annual Percentage Change—Years Ended 12/31*

	Windsor Fund	S&P 500		Windsor Fund	S&P 500
1958	+ 4.2%	+ 8.6%	1975	+54.5	+37.1
1959	+16.4	+11.9	1976	+46.4	+23.8
1960	+11.2	+ 0.4	1977	+ 1.0	− 7.2
1961	+29.6	+26.9	1978	+ 8.8	+ 6.5
1962	−25.0	− 8.7	1979	+22.6	+18.4
1963	+12.7	+22.8	1980	+22.6	+32.4
1964	+13.9	+16.4	1981	+16.8	− 4.9
1965	−29.1	+12.5	1982	+21.7	+21.5
1966	− 3.3	−10.0	1983	+30.1	+22.5
1967	+31.5	+23.9	1984	+19.5	+ 6.2
1968	+21.4	+11.0	1985	+28.0	+31.6
1969	− 3.8	− 8.4	1986	+20.3	+18.6
1970	+ 6.4	+ 3.9	1987	+ 1.2	+ 5.2
1971	+ 7.5	+14.2	1988	+28.7	+16.5
1972	+10.2	+19.0	1989	+15.0	+31.6
1973	−25.0	−14.7	1990	−15.5	− 3.1
1974	−16.8	−26.3	1991	+28.5	+30.3

*Adjusted to include reinvestment of income dividends and capital gains distributions for both the fund and index.

Source: Reprinted by permission of The Vanguard Group.

Keep in mind that when investing for growth, current income is not a high priority. All numbers in Figure 11.2 reflect total return, which assumes that income dividends and capital gains distributions have been reinvested into additional shares. The number of funds represented in each group range from as few as 32 (precious metals) to as many as 305 (long-term growth).

Figure 11.2 corroborates a basic principle of investing. There is a direct correlation between risk and reward: The greater the risk, the greater the potential reward. Funds that invest in common stocks generally have experienced significantly higher long-term results (see the total return column for 10 years) than have funds that invest primarily in bonds. However, note that the riskier maximum capital gain and small-company growth groups did worse than the more conservatively managed long-term growth, growth and income and

FIGURE 11.2   Average Investment Performance

Total Return
(For the Period Ending December 31, 1991)

Mutual Fund Classification	1 Year	5 Years	10 Years	Avg. Yield Last 12 Months
Maximum capital gain	42.8%	97.8%	306.3%	1.1%
Small-company growth	51.9	107.2	270.3	0.5
Long-term growth	35.8	87.0	319.3	1.5
Growth and income	27.4	76.6	322.3	2.4
Balanced	24.0	68.4	337.0	3.8
Income—stocks	25.0	58.5	301.6	4.3
Flexible policy	26.8	54.8	263.3	5.5
Corporate bonds	16.2	52.9	249.1	7.3
Corporate high-yield bonds	35.7	36.2	201.3	11.4
International—stocks	13.7	57.9	307.5	1.4
Precious metals	−4.9	3.5	44.4	0.9
U.S. government securities	14.3	50.5	210.1	6.9
Tax-exempt bonds	11.2	42.2	228.8	5.9
Utilities	20.8	63.2	371.1	5.4

Source: CDA/Wiesenberger Investment Companies Service.

balanced groups. In extended time periods, the reverse would be expected. In the debt-oriented funds, corporate bonds and tax-exempt categories outperformed U.S. government securities. This would be expected due to the lower risk level of government securities.

Another interesting fact is that there is frequently an inverse relationship between a fund's current yield and the long-term growth it realizes. The groups with the lowest average yields (maximum capital gain, long-term growth, international stocks, growth and income and balanced) produced the highest ten-year returns. Conversely, the corporate high-yield bonds, corporate bonds and U.S. government securities groups produced the worst long-term growth.

Next we'll look at some of the fund classifications, their investment objectives and policies and how some of the best funds in each group have performed. The performance figures shown for individual funds are for the periods ending December 31, 1991. Incidentally, a fund's investment objective refers to that which the fund seeks to accomplish for its shareowners, while its investment policies set forth the means, or management techniques, by which it hopes to attain its objective.

Maximum Capital Gain

Funds included in this category are those with investment objectives and policies that reflect a willingness to accept a substantial amount of risk. Their objectives might state that they seek aggressive growth or maximum capital appreciation. Investment policies may include investment in small or emerging companies, the use of leverage (much as a home buyer leverages his or her funds by taking out a mortgage) and other speculative investment techniques. (See Figure 11.3.)

Just because a fund falls into the maximum capital gain classification does not mean it will attain substantial growth. Some funds are successfully managed and many others are not. Interestingly, some funds that are included in lower-risk groups will have long-term records that outperform funds in the maximum capital gain group.

Long-Term Growth

By far the largest number of funds fall into the long-term growth category. Funds in this group have long-term growth of capital as their primary investment objective. Current income, although not ignored,

FIGURE 11.3   Top-Performing Funds in the Maximum Capital Gain Classification

(For the Period Ending December 31, 1991)

Fund	1 Year	5 Years	10 Years	Avg. Yield Last 12 Months
Acorn Fund	47.3%	97.8%	366.6%	1.1%
Evergreen Fund	40.1	69.7	304.0	1.2
Nicholas Fund	41.9	98.2	431.2	1.4
Pennsylvania Mutual Fund	32.5	72.8	370.9	2.3
Twentieth Century Growth Investors	69.0	170.3	419.6	0.1

Source: CDA/Wiesenberger Investment Companies Service.

FIGURE 11.4   Top-Performing Funds in the Long-Term
Growth Classification

(For the Period Ending December 31, 1991)

Fund	1 Year	5 Years	10 Years	Avg. Yield Last 12 Months
Ivy Growth Fund	30.8%	76.8%	401.2%	1.5%
Janus Fund	42.1	150.7	477.4	1.0
Stein Roe Special Fund	34.0	118.2	486.5	1.8
Twentieth Century Select Investors	31.4	103.9	461.8	1.5
Vanguard Windsor Fund	30.0	64.6	379.5	6.1

Source: CDA/Wiesenberger Investment Companies Service.

is of secondary importance. Investments usually will be in common stocks. However, a lower level of risk is accepted by funds in this group than is taken by funds seeking growth in a more aggressive manner (such as those included in the maximum capital gain group).

Growth and Income

Long-term growth of capital and income and a reasonable current return is an objective that would typify funds in this classification. The production of current income that will grow over the years is part of what these funds try to achieve. While common stocks frequently predominate, bonds and preferred stocks also play an important role. Risk will be controlled by investing mainly in large, well-capitalized companies with long-term growth in earnings and dividends. (See Figure 11.5.)

Balanced Funds

A balanced fund approaches the investment of its assets as if they constitute the complete investment program of an investor who wants to conserve his or her principal and purchasing power, receive current income and seek long-term growth of both principal and income. Up to 75 percent of investments will normally be in high-quality common

FIGURE 11.5   Top-Performing Funds in the Growth and
Income Classification

(For the Period Ending December 31, 1991

Fund	1 Year	5 Years	10 Years	Avg. Yield Last 12 Months
Dodge & Cox Stock Fund	21.5%	86.4%	393.9%	3.0%
Elfun Trusts	28.1	105.3	405.5	2.6
Evergreen Total Return Fund	22.9	41.5	318.8	5.6
Selected American Shares	46.3	106.4	459.9	1.3
Stein Roe Total Return Fund	29.6	66.5	263.0	4.8
Vanguard Index Trust 500	30.2	101.2	385.8	2.9

Source: CDA/Wiesenberger Investment Companies Service.

and preferred stocks, with the balance in corporate bonds and cash equivalents. (See Figure 11.6.)

Income—Stocks

The primary objective of funds in this group is to seek income, but capital growth may be pursued where it is consistent with the primary objective. The emphasis is ordinarily on common stocks and securities convertible into common stocks. But the funds may also invest in nonconvertible preferred stocks, bonds and debentures. (See Figure 11.7.)

FIGURE 11.6   Top-Performing Funds in the Balanced
Fund Classification

(For the Period Ending December 31, 1991)

Fund	1 Year	5 Years	10 Years	Avg. Yield Last 12 Months
CGM Mutual Fund	40.9%	103.3%	463.5%	3.3%
Dodge & Cox Balanced Fund	20.7	79.2	335.9	4.5
Strong Investment Fund	19.6	48.8	343.8	4.8
Vanguard Wellington Fund	23.7	73.6	350.0	5.0

Source: CDA/Wiesenberger Investment Companies Service.

FIGURE 11.7   Top-Performing Funds in the Income-Stocks Classification

(For the Period Ending December 31, 1991)

Fund	1 Year	5 Years	10 Years	Avg. Yield Last 12 Months
Mairs & Power Income Fund	25.9%	73.9%	309.3%	3.7%
SAFECO Income Fund	23.3	46.7	301.3	5.1

Source: CDA/Wiesenberger Investment Companies Service.

Flexible Policy

As the title implies, the funds in this group have somewhat flexible policies. Their objective is generally to provide income as high and dependable as is consistent with reasonable risk. Investments may be in common or preferred stocks, bonds or other securities, in any proportions. The selection of securities will depend on which investments management believes offer the best opportunities for income (and secondarily for capital growth). (See Figure 11.8.)

FIGURE 11.8   Top-Performing Funds in the Flexible Policy Classification

(For the Period Ending December 31, 1991)

Fund	1 Year	5 Years	10 Years	Avg. Yield Last 12 Months
Fidelity Puritan Fund	24.5%	62.8%	354.7%	5.5%
Nicholas Income Fund	23.0	44.8	234.8	10.4
Value Line Income Fund	29.6	77.4	264.6	4.7
Vanguard Wellesley Income Fund	21.5	69.9	336.9	7.0

Source: CDA/Wiesenberger Investment Companies Service.

Corporate Bonds

The primary objective of funds included in the corporate bond groups is generally to earn a high level of current income. They do this by investing in fixed-income corporate securities of various types, including bonds, debentures and preferred stocks. The quality will vary depending on the specific objective and investment policies of each individual fund. Some funds seek a higher level of income by investing in lower-grade (junk) bonds. This increases current income but subjects a fund to substantial risk in the event of an economic recession. (See Figure 11.9.)

International

Some funds in the international category have enjoyed good returns in the last several years during a period of surging foreign securities markets. The investment objective of these funds is long-term capital growth. They generally invest only in the stocks of companies domiciled outside the United States. (See Figure 11.10.)

Precious Metals

Funds in this group seek long-term capital appreciation; income is secondary. The policy of the funds is to invest principally in the equities

FIGURE 11.9   Top-Performing Funds in the Corporate
Bonds Classification

(For the Period Ending December 31, 1991)

Fund	1 Year	5 Years	10 Years	Avg. Yield Last 12 Months
Dreyfus A Bonds Plus	18.8%	54.4%	232.2%	7.5%
Fidelity Flexible Bond Fund	18.9	53.8	227.8	8.1
Keystone Custodian Series—B1	14.9	41.1	218.9	7.6
T. Rowe Price New Income Fund	15.5	54.8	215.9	7.4
Vanguard Fixed Income Investment Grade Bond	20.9	62.6	255.6	8.0

Source: CDA/Wiesenberger Investment Companies Service.

FIGURE 11.10   Top-Performing Funds in the International
Classification

(For the Period Ending December 31, 1991)

Fund	1 Year	5 Years	10 Years	Avg. Yield Last 12 Months
Keystone International Fund	14.2%	15.2%	182.5%	3.9%
Kleinworth Benson				
International Equity Fund	11.8	55.0	248.9	4.1
Scudder International Fund	11.8	55.0	351.1	0.0
Vanguard World International	4.7	44.3	184.5	1.8

Source: CDA/Wiesenberger Investment Companies Service.

of companies engaged in the mining, processing or dealing in gold or
other precious metals. Precious metals funds have generally fared
poorly in the last five years, but some did very well before that. (See
Figure 11.11.)

Industry

Long-term growth of principal and income is the primary investment
objective of funds in this group. They generally invest in the equity
securities of companies engaged in a particular industry such as mining, technology, insurance, banks, energy, utilities, etc. There are

FIGURE 11.11   Top-Performing Funds in the Precious Metals
Classification

(For the Period Ending December 31, 1991)

Fund	1 Year	5 Years	10 Years	Avg. Yield Last 12 Months
Bull & Bear Gold Investors				
Limited	− 1.1%	3.6%	14.6%	0.4%
Keystone Precious Metals	8.2	19.9	48.8	0.8
United Services Gold Shares	−15.6	−22.7	−4.3	2.9

Source: CDA/Wiesenberger Investment Companies Service.

FIGURE 11.12   Top-Performing Funds in the Industry Classification

(For the Period Ending December 31, 1991)

Fund	1 Year	5 Years	10 Years	Avg. Yield Last 12 Months
Century Shares Trust	28.0%	78.1%	334.4%	2.2%
Fidelity Select Financial Services	61.6	36.5	348.6	0.9
Neuberger Berman Selected Sectors	24.7	78.4	210.7	1.7

Source: CDA/Wiesenberger Investment Companies Service.

relatively few no-load mutual funds in this classification that have been in operation long enough to have ten-year performance records. (See Figure 11.12.)

U.S. Government Securities

Funds in this group invest only in securities that are obligations of the U.S. government or its agencies. The investment objective is current income. In terms of total return, the experience of these funds generally has been mediocre, at best, but quite good for current income. (See Figure 11.13.)

Tax-Exempt Bonds

The objective of all funds in this category is to produce current income that is exempt from federal income taxes. The funds do this by investing in tax-free municipal bonds issued by the various states (and Puerto Rico) and their agencies. Many fund groups offer individual state portfolios, income from which is also exempt from the taxes of the particular state whose municipal bonds they hold.

Tax-exempt funds control risk by maintaining a certain level of quality and length of maturity of the bonds they hold. The more conservative funds invest only in investment-grade bonds (those in the top three rating categories) and those with short or intermediate

FIGURE 11.13   Top-Performing Funds in the U.S. Government
Securities Classification

(For the Period Ending December 31, 1991)

Fund	1 Year	5 Years	10 Years	Avg. Yield Last 12 Months
Fund For U.S. Government Securities	13.3%	59.7%	255.1%	8.1%
Lexington GNMA Income Fund	15.7	58.8	217.8	7.6
Mutual of Omaha America	15.4	55.0	175.9	6.6
Value Line U.S. Government Securities	16.4	60.6	247.5	7.4
Vanguard Fixed Income GNMA	16.8	64.3	264.3	7.9

Source: CDA/Wiesenberger Investment Companies Service.

maturities. The high-yield bond funds invest in lower-rated or nonrated
bonds and those of longer maturities.

While there are now a large number of tax-exempt mutual funds,
there are relatively few with a ten-year performance history. This is
because it was not until 1976 that legislation was passed by Congress
that permitted investment companies to pass through the federal tax-
exempt income feature of municipal bonds. (See Figure 11.14.)

FIGURE 11.14   Top-Performing Funds in the Tax-Exempt
Bonds Classification

(For the Period Ending December 31, 1991)

Fund	1 Year	5 Years	10 Years	Avg. Yield Last 12 Months
Elfun Tax-Exempt Fund	12.1%	47.0%	323.8%	6.3%
Fidelity High Yield Tax-Fee Portfolio	10.2	45.2	253.0	6.6
Keystone Tax Free Fund	10.8	41.2	229.0	6.5
Stein Roe Managed Municipals	11.9	47.3	295.7	6.0
Vanguard Municipal Bond High Yield	14.7	51.2	259.5	6.9

Source: CDA/Wiesenberger Investment Companies Service.

FIGURE 11.15   Best-Performing No-Load Mutual Funds

(For Periods Ending December 31, 1991)

Fund	1 Year
CGM Capital Development Fund	99.2%
Financial Strategic Health Sciences	91.7
Berger 100 Fund	88.8
Twentieth Century Ultra Investors	86.4
Twentieth Century Giftrust Investors	84.6
Kaufmann Fund	79.5
MIM Stock Appreciation	76.9
Financial Strategic Technology	76.8
Financial Strategic Financial Services	74.7
	5 Years
Financial Strategic Health Sciences	378.0%
Twentieth Century Ultra Investors	237.5
Berger 100 Fund	211.0
Vanguard Specialized Health Care	190.2
Twentieth Century Giftrust Investors	177.9
CGM Capital Development Fund	175.2
Twentieth Century Growth Investors	170.2
Janus Twenty Fund	169.8
	10 Years
CGM Capital Development Fund	882.0%
Financial Industrial Income Fund	525.6
Twentieth Century Ultra Investors	523.3
IAI Regional Fund	497.9
Sequoia Fund	489.5
Stein Roe Special Fund	486.5

Source: CDA/Wiesenberger Investment Companies Service.

One thing to remember about tax-free bond funds is that while the income distributions are exempt from taxes, any realized capital gains are not. There are not many capital gains distributions from tax-exempt bond funds (which are taxable), but if you sell your shares for a price that is greater than your cost, the profit of course is subject to income tax.

TOP-PERFORMING NO-LOAD MUTUAL FUNDS

Figure 11.15 lists the best-performing no-load mutual funds during the one-, five- and ten-year periods ending on December 31, 1991. Keep in mind that past performance is not necessarily an indication of future performance. Last year's "hot" fund may be a laggard this year, but funds that perform well over extended periods of time should be thoughtfully considered. To get complete information, call the specific fund for a prospectus.

SUMMARY

Without question, mutual funds provide an excellent means for building wealth. Common sense and patience are essential, both in evaluating and selecting funds to buy as well as during the period that you hold the funds and wait for the gradual growth of your capital. When investing in mutual funds for the purpose of capital appreciation, always reinvest both your dividend and capital gains distributions.

The evidence seems to indicate that well-managed funds that are not hampered by restrictive and limiting investment policies tend to produce the best long-term results. Finally, if a fund's yield from dividend distributions is high, its long-term total returns will generally be lower.

CHAPTER 12

Investing for Income

Nearly everyone wants more income, whether to supplement what's already coming in, to accumulate assets for the future or for some other purpose. Mutual funds provide a simple and convenient way to meet this need. Cash assets, large or small, can be invested in funds whose only purpose is to deliver regular cash distributions.

But as in all investing, there are pitfalls. The investor should always remember that as a general rule, the higher the return, the greater the risk. There's just no way to get around this basic principle, although there are occasional exceptions.

NO-LOAD VERSUS LOAD FUNDS

One simple way to obtain a higher yield without increasing your risk is to select an income fund with no sales charge or 12b-1 distribution fees and also one that has low annual expenses. Assuming equivalent management competence, investment objectives and operating policies of the mutual funds under consideration, the result will be a higher distribution of income to you. Here's an example of how this works for a $10,000 investment:

$10,000 Invested at $10.00 Per Share (Net Asset Value)

	Sales Charge*	Offering Price	Shares Bought
Fund A	4.5%	$10.47	955.11
Fund B	0.0	10.00	1,000.00

Income Distribution

	Annual Expenses**	Per Share	Annual Income	Yield
Fund A	1.0%	$0.90	$859.60	8.6%
Fund B	0.5	0.95	950.00	9.5

*As a percentage of the offering price.
**Both funds A and B are assumed to develop a 10 percent income from invested assets, before expenses.

It is clear from this illustration that sales charges and expense ratios can have a dramatic impact on mutual fund yields.

TAX-FREE INCOME

Your first decision in seeking to develop current income is to determine whether you want the income to be tax-free or taxable. The after-tax return on high-yielding taxable funds may provide you with less money to keep after taxes than you will have from lower-yielding tax-free funds. A little simple arithmetic will help you determine which is better for you.

For example, if you pay 28 percent of your income in taxes to Uncle Sam, you will keep 72 percent. Thus, if a taxable fund is paying out dividends at a 10 percent annual distribution rate, you will be left with 7.2 percent after taxes. You would need to get more than 7.2 percent tax-free to beat the 10 percent taxable rate.

If you live in a state that has an income tax, the value of tax-free income becomes even more important. Normally, to avoid state income taxes on its dividends, a fund may only invest in municipal bonds issued in that state (and in most cases, Puerto Rico). Several fund groups offer funds that hold only single-state municipal bonds. The income from such funds will be exempt from both federal and state taxes (of the designated state).

Figure 12.1 illustrates how the benefits of tax-free income grow with your tax bracket. An investor in the maximum 33 percent federal income-tax bracket must earn a return of 10.45 percent from a fully taxable investment to equal a 7 percent yield that is exempt from federal income taxes. To see how this applies to you, locate your income tax bracket and then read across the chart to find the equivalent taxable yield you need to match the tax-free yield at various rates.

Tax-free income funds are generally offered in several levels of quality and lengths of maturity. The quality relates to the creditworthiness of the bonds in the portfolio, such as investment-grade, medium-grade, low-grade (junk) or insured bonds. Maturities are generally grouped into short-, intermediate- and long-term lengths. The Vanguard Group, for example, offers the Vanguard Municipal Bond Fund, which is composed of seven portfolios offering tax-free income that is payable monthly:

1. Municipal Money Market Portfolio—Invests primarily in investment-grade municipal securities and expects to maintain an average weighted maturity of 120 days or less. The net asset value (NAV) is expected to remain constant at $1 per share. Principal risk is minimal.
2. Muncipal Bond Short Term Portfolio—Offers a high degree of capital stability with an average weighted maturity of one to two years. Price fluctuations and principal risk should be low.
3. Municipal Limited Term Portfolio—Seeks yields higher than those of short-term bonds but with less price volatility than long-term bonds. It invests in high-quality municipal bonds and expects to maintain an average weighted maturity of two to five years. Price fluctuations and principal risk should be moderate.
4. Municipal Bond Intermediate Term Portfolio—Invests in high-quality municipal bonds and expects to maintain an average maturity of 7 to 12 years. Price fluctuations and principal risk are moderate to high.
5. Municipal Insured Long Term Portfolio—Invests in high-quality municipal bonds that are covered by insurance guaranteeing the timely payment of principal and interest. The average weighted maturity is expected to be 20 to 25 years. Credit risk is virtually eliminated, but principal is subject to a high degree of price fluctuations.
6. Municipal Bond Long Term Portfolio—Invests in high-quality, long-term municipal bonds and expects to maintain an average

FIGURE 12.1   Example of How the Benefits of Tax-Free Income
Grow with Your Tax Bracket

Tax Bracket	Tax-Free Yields				
	6.50%	7.00%	7.50%	8.00%	8.50%
	Equivalent Taxable Yields				
15%	7.65%	8.24%	8.82%	9.41%	10.00%
28	9.03	9.72	10.42	11.11	11.81
33	9.70	10.45	11.19	11.94	12.69

weighted maturity of 20 to 25 years. There is high potential for price fluctuations and risk to principal.

7. Municipal Bond High Yield Portfolio—Invests primarily in medium-quality municipal bonds and expects to maintain an average weighted maturity of 20 to 25 years. This portfolio pursues the highest yields of the group and has a high potential for price fluctuations and risk to principal.

It is easy to get the current yields or annualized dividend distribution rates of any individual fund, either by calling the fund directly (usually on their toll-free number) or by looking it up yourself in a good financial periodical, such as *Barron's*.

Barron's lists the most recent dividend paid (as well as for the last 12 months) and the NAV for each fund listed. To determine the current dividend distribution rate, simply multiply the last dividend paid by the number of payments made per year (usually 12) and divide that by the NAV per share. On that basis, the distribution rates for the preceding Vanguard Municipal Bond Fund Portfolios funds on February 10, 1992, were as follows:

Municipal Money Market Portfolio	3.23%
Municipal Bond Short Term Portfolio	4.66
Municipal Limited Term Portfolio	5.18
Municipal Bond Intermediate Term Portfolio	5.98
Municipal Insured Long Term Portfolio	6.59
Municipal Bond Long Term Portfolio	6.89
Municipal Bond High Yield Portfolio	7.06

Source: Reprinted by permission of *Barron's,* © 1992 Dow Jones & Company, Inc. All Rights Reserved Worldwide.

TAXABLE INCOME

There is a diverse group of funds whose investment objectives are dedicated primarily to the development of current income that is not tax-exempt. They fall into two general categories: (1) those holding securities issued or backed by the U.S. government (or its agencies) and (2) those issued by domestic corporations or foreign companies and governments.

Each of the major mutual fund groups offers several types of funds where the primary investment objective is distribution of income. For comparative illustration, several funds offered by the Fidelity Investments Group are listed below.

Money Market Funds

The NAV of each fund remains fixed at $1.
- Cash Reserves—Seeks to obtain as high a level of income as is consistent with the preservation of capital and liquidity. It invests in high-grade domestic and international money market instruments.
- Daily Income—The same as Cash Reserves except that it invests only in domestic money market instruments.
- Spartan Money—Seeks the highest money market yields wherever they may be. It invests in U.S. dollar-denominated money market securities at home or overseas.
- U.S. Government Reserves—Seeks as high a level of income as is consistent with the security of principal and liquidity by investing in instruments issued or guaranteed as to principal and interest by the U.S. government, its agencies or instrumentalities. All investments are in obligations that mature in one year or less.

Fixed Income Funds

- Flexible Bond Fund—Seeks to obtain a high rate of return, with capital appreciation possibilities where appropriate, through investment in a broad range of fixed-income securities. Investments are to be consistent with reasonable risk.
- High-Income Fund—Seeks to earn a high level of current income through investment in a diversified portfolio consisting primarily of high-yielding (lower-grade) fixed-income corporate securities.

- Intermediate Bond Fund—Seeks a high level of current income by investing in high-grade fixed-income obligations. The portfolio will have an average maturity of three to ten years.
- GNMA Portfolio—Invests primarily in mortgage-related securities issued by the Government National Mortgage Association (GNMA) and other obligations guaranteed as to payment of principal and interest by the U.S. government. It seeks a high level of current income, consistent with prudent investment risk.
- Government Securities —Seeks a high level of current income consistent with preservation of capital. The fund invests only in U.S. government and government agency securities that provide interest that is specifically exempted from state and local income taxes when held directly by taxpayers.
- Mortgage Securities Fund—Seeks a high level of current income consistent with prudent investment risk. It invests primarily in a broad range of mortgage-related securities issued by governmental, government-related and private organizations.
- Short-Term Bond Portfolio—Seeks high current income consistent with preservation of capital by investing primarily in a broad range of investment-grade fixed-income securities. The fund will maintain an average maturity of three years or less.

All income distributions on these funds are payable monthly. Their dividend distribution rates (yields) as of March 2, 1992 were as follows:

Cash Reserves	4.35%
Daily Income	4.07
Spartan Money	4.57
U.S. Government Reserves	4.07
Flexible Bond Fund	8.21
High Income Fund	11.26
Intermediate Bond Fund	7.28
GNMA Portfolio	7.41
Government Securities	7.63
Mortgage Securities Fund	7.48
Short-Term Bond Portfolio	8.75

Funds offered by other mutual fund groups having investment objectives that match the preceding funds will have similar yields. While there can be some differences in managements' ability to acquire securities efficiently, and thus increase yield, the most effective ways for a fund to produce a higher yield is by controlling its costs or by purchasing lower-quality securities. (Generally speaking, the less creditworthy a security is, the higher will be its yield.)

HIGHEST-YIELDING NO-LOAD MUTUAL FUNDS

Figure 12.2 identifies the highest-yielding no-load mutual funds as of December 31, 1991, in each of several investment objective categories where income is primary. Funds with annual 12b-1 fees exceeding 0.25% are not included.

FIGURE 12.2   Highest-Yielding No-Load Mutual Funds by Investment Objective as of December 31, 1991

Fund	Yield
Equity Income	
Vanguard Preferred Stock Fund	7.9%
Flexible Income	
Nicholas Income	10.4
Fidelity Capital & Income Fund	10.2
Janus Flexible Income Fund	9.8
Corporate Bond	
GE S&S Long Term Interest Fund	14.9
Berwyn Income Fund	9.1
Scudder Short Term Bond	8.9
Corporate High Yield	
Northeast Investors Trust	14.7
Government Mortgage	
Dreyfus GNMA Fund	8.7
Municipal Bond	
Sit New Beginning Tax-Free Income Fund	7.3
General Municipal Bond Fund	7.2

Source: CDA/Wiesenberger Investment Companies Service.

SUMMARY

Mutual funds provide excellent financial vehicles for the investor seeking income. First, the value-conscious investor will generally buy funds with no sales charges (either front-end or back-end loads) and no significant 12b-1 fees. Next, determine if you might get a higher after-tax return by investing in tax-exempt funds. Your tolerance for risk and the extent of market fluctuations you are willing to accept will influence the type of fund you purchase. Finally, check the prospectus (usually on page 3) for the fund's record of maintaining a consistent dividend payout and holding up the level of its NAV per share.

CHAPTER 13

Balancing Growth and Income

As we pointed out in Chapter 9, "How To Start an Investment Program," the best approach to investing for most people is to maintain a balanced portfolio. This calls for keeping a relatively fixed amount of funds distributed among equities, debt and cash equivalents. There are two ways for the mutual fund investor to do this.

First, determine the portfolio mix that is appropriate for you (e.g., 60 percent in common stocks, 25 percent in bonds and 15 percent in money market securities). Then select one or more soundly managed funds with good past performance records for investment in each category. For the best control and flexibility, use one mutual fund group for the funds you choose. That way you can shift assets easily and quickly from one fund category to another if you decide to change your allocation percentages. To achieve greater diversification, and if the amount of your assets warrants it, invest in two or more fund families, using the same proportions among fund types in each group.

Second, invest in a *balanced fund*. See Appendix A ("No-Load Mutual Funds—by Investment Objective") for a list of no-load balanced funds.

BALANCED FUNDS

The easy way to achieve a prudently balanced investment portfolio is to buy shares in one of the so-called balanced funds. They hold, at all times, a portion of their assets in bonds and/or preferred stocks, as

FIGURE 13.1   Statistical History of Wellington Fund

Year	Net Asset Value	Annual Dividend	Yield from Dividends	Capital Gains Distribution
1991	$18.80	$ .96	5.1%	$.23
1990	16.26	1.01	6.2%	.00
1989	17.78	1.02	5.5%	.60
1988	16.01	.96	5.8%	.58
1987	15.15	.98	6.4%	.14
1986	15.85	.94	5.8%	.34
1985	14.50	.92	6.2%	.30
1984	12.32	.92	7.2%	.48
1983	12.46	.91	7.1%	.44
1982	11.21	.87	7.8%	–

Source: CDA/Wiesenberger Investment Companies Service.

well as in common stocks and other equity-type securities. The balanced funds treat the monies under their control as if their shareholders have entrusted the fund managers with their entire investable assets. They intend to provide a complete investment program in a single financial vehicle. The objective of a balanced fund is to minimize investment risks as much as possible without sacrificing the potential for long-term growth of capital and current income.

VANGUARD WELLINGTON FUND, INC.

An outstanding example of a balanced fund is the Wellington Fund, the oldest and one of the largest members of the Vanguard group of investment companies. It was founded on December 29, 1929, and has become one of the nation's largest balanced funds. The fund is managed by the Wellington Management Company, which is not affiliated with the Vanguard Group.

The investment objectives of the fund include conservation of principal, reasonable income return and profits without undue risk. As of November 30, 1991, the fund was invested 60 percent in common stocks and 40 percent in debt instruments. (Cash and cash equivalents were negligible.) The common stock holdings were in five major industry groups: (1) applied science and research, (2) basic industry, (3) finance, (4) consumer and services and (5) utilities. Its largest individual stock positions were in Bristol Mycrs Squibb, General Electric, DuPont (E.I.) de Nemours, Exxon, Kimberly Clark and Norwest.

The annual yield from income dividends paid out to shareowners has ranged from a low of 5.1 percent (in 1991) to a high of 7.8 percent (in 1982) during the ten years ending in 1991. Actual dividends paid per share increased over the years from $.87 a share in 1982 to $.96 a share in 1991. In early 1992 the current dividend distribution rate (yield) was 4.3 percent. Additionally, the fund made capital gains distributions totaling $3.11 over the ten-year period. (See Figure 13.1.)

It is interesting to note that the $.96 per share dividend paid in 1991 represents a yield of 8.6 percent on the original investment at $11.21 net asset value (NAV) per share in 1982. And this does not take into account the capital gains distributions that presumably would have been reinvested in additional shares. Figure 13.2 shows an example of an assumed investment of $10,000 in the Wellington Fund.

FIGURE 13.2   An Assumed Investment of $10,000 in the Wellington Fund on January 1, 1981

Year	Total Value*	Income Dividends
1981	$10,290	$ 832
1982	12,817	942
1983	15,838	1,066
1984	17,532	1,199
1985	22,534	1,339
1986	26,681	1,492
1987	27,287	1,682
1988	31,683	1,766
1989	38,528	2,060
1990	37,447	2,237

*Total value of shares on December 31, with all dividends and capital gains reinvested.

FIGURE 13.3   Approximate Total Return, with All Dividends and Capital Gains Reinvested (For Years Ending 12/31/91)

	1 Year	5 Years	10 Years
CGM Mutual Fund	40.9%	103.3%	463.5%
Dodge & Cox Balanced Fund	20.7	79.2	335.9
Pax World Fund	20.7	90.6	310.1
State Farm Balanced Fund	39.2	131.1	426.4
USF&G Axe-Houghton Fund B	22.1	66.2	305.8

Source: CDA/Wiesenberger Investment Companies Service.

OTHER BALANCED FUNDS

While only about 2 percent of all mutual funds can be categorized as balanced funds, a number of no-load funds have had good track records and have been in operation long enough for their performances to be meaningful. (See Figure 13.3.)

SUMMARY

Balanced funds represent a conservative approach for the mutual fund investor who wants to maintain a balanced portfolio. Nearly all large investors, such as pension funds, endowments, institutions and wealthy individuals, balance their funds between equities, debt and cash equivalents. The beauty of a balanced fund is that it represents a complete investment program in a single security.

CHAPTER 14

Using the All-Time Favorite Investment Technique

Few investment techniques have stood the test of time to the extent that one can confidently say "This works." But there is such a method. It is easy, it works and you can do it. It is called *dollar cost averaging* and is simply the practice of buying securities at regular intervals in fixed dollar amounts, regardless of price levels.

Many mutual fund investors build up their shareholder accounts through such systematic purchases over long periods of time. These investors may add as little as $25 a month to their accounts, or they may be company retirement plans that invest millions of dollars each year. Both take advantage of dollar cost averaging, one of the simplest and most effective ways of building an investment account that has ever been developed.

When this procedure is followed, more shares of stock are purchased at relatively low prices than at high prices. As a result, the average cost of all shares bought turns out to be lower than the average of all the prices at which purchases were made. The combination of buying shares at a variety of price levels and acquiring more shares at low rather than high prices has proven to be an efficient and cost-effective method of accumulating securities.

AVERAGE COST VERSUS AVERAGE PRICE

The arithmetic that illustrates how dollar cost averaging works is simple. The investor need remember only that by periodically purchasing shares with identical amounts of money, as long as there is any change in share prices at all during the investment period, the average cost of shares purchased will be less than the average of the prices paid. Assume that $280 is the regular amount to be invested. A series of five purchases totaling $1,400 is made at prices varying between $10 and $5 a share. The number of shares bought for each $280 purchase would be as follows:

Price	Shares Purchased
$10	28
8	35
7	40
5	56
8	35

Total shares acquired for $1,400 investment: 194.
Average cost of each share ($1,400 divided by 194): $7.21.
Average price of shares purchased: $7.60.

The principle that makes this program work is that equal numbers of dollars buy more shares at low prices than at high prices. It is essential that purchases be made at low prices when they are available. The investor contemplating dollar cost averaging must take into account his or her emotional and financial ability to continue making new investments through periods of low price levels.

The use of dollar cost averaging does not guarantee that the investor will always have profits in his or her account or that he or she will never incur losses. A share accumulation program of this type should be used only for long-term purposes. The investor should feel confident that the invested funds will not be needed for a considerable number of years.

The risks inherent in securities investing are substantially reduced through dollar cost averaging. This is because shares are bound to be purchased over the years at a variety of price levels—high, low and in between. That fact alone should provide a better income and capital gains experience than haphazard investing or buying only when the outlook appears bright.

GROWTH IS NOT ESSENTIAL

Fluctuating security prices are more important to successful dollar cost averaging than long-term growth alone. This surprising fact arises because it is actually during periods of declining prices that the investor gets his or her best opportunity to acquire a large number of shares.

Continuing with the previous example, assume that after the five purchases had been made, the share price returned to $10, the level of the first purchase. The 194 shares already owned would have a value of $1,940. During the purchase period, note that a 50 percent decline in price was assumed to have taken place.

Now, instead of a drop in price, let's see what would happen if the share price had steadily advanced to an increase of 50 percent and the five equal purchases of $280 were made, again until the full $1,400 was invested.

Price	Shares Purchased
$10	28.00
11	25.45
12	23.33
14	20.00
15	18.67

Shares acquired by $1,400 investment: 115.45.
Average cost of each share ($1,400 divided by 115.45): $12.13.
Average price of shares that were purchased: $12.40.

In this example, the process of dollar cost averaging also results in an average cost that is less than the average price. But notice that after a 50 percent increase from the initial price of $10 per share, the total value of the 115.45 shares at $15 is $1,731.75, or about 11.7 percent less than the $1,940 that the 194 shares in the previous example were worth at $10.

Of course, the investor has no control over the direction security prices will take once he or she starts a dollar cost averaging program. But the main advantage of the plan is that in the long run it will work to the investor's benefit almost regardless of what the market does. This fact is particularly important to the investor who fears starting an investment program because he or she believes stock prices are too high. If the investor is right and the market does decline, the timing may be just right to begin dollar cost averaging.

REINVESTING INCOME AND CAPITAL GAINS DISTRIBUTIONS

Most investors who invest in securities on a periodic basis can and do reinvest any distributions they receive. The effect in the beginning is minor, but as the program continues the impact of compounding shares becomes more and more significant. The relative importance will vary, of course, depending on the emphasis that a particular fund places on producing income distributions.

While it is not necessary that income dividends be reinvested for dollar cost averaging to work, the reinvestment of capital gains distributions is most important. The reason is that capital gains distributions represent a return of principal. Thus, taking them in cash has the effect of reducing an investor's capital.

DOLLAR COST AVERAGING AT WORK

To illustrate the value of a long-term investment program using dollar cost averaging, Figure 14.1 shows the hypothetical results of investing $2,000 in the Standard & Poor's (S&P) 500 Index on January 1st of each year for 33 years, beginning in 1959 and continuing through 1991. It is assumed that all dividends are reinvested.

The annual amount of $2,000 was chosen since it is the maximum allowable individual retirement account (IRA) contribution for an individual participant under current law. With no income taxes required to be paid on dividends or capital gains accumulating in an IRA, the IRA is an ideal vehicle for a dollar cost averaging plan.

The widely known S&P 500 Index has been used because it is generally recognized as representing overall price trends among a wide segment of well-known industrial common stocks. Since it is simply a list of the stocks of 500 large companies and is subject to no expenses or costs of operation, the index is not strictly comparable to the shares of any mutual fund.

FIGURE 14.1   Example of Investing $2,000 Annually for 33 Years in the S&P 500

Year	Total Amount Invested	Total Value of Account
1959	$ 2,000	$ 2,238
1960	4,000	4,254
1961	6,000	7,937
1962	8,000	9,072
1963	10,000	13,597
1964	12,000	18,155
1965	14,000	22,675
1966	16,000	22,207
1967	18,000	29,993
1968	20,000	35,512
1969	22,000	34,361
1970	24,000	37,779
1971	26,000	45,427
1972	28,000	56,439
1973	30,000	49,848
1974	32,000	38,212
1975	34,000	55,131
1976	36,000	70,728
1977	38,000	67,492
1978	40,000	74,009
1979	42,000	89,994
1980	44,000	121,801
1981	46,000	117,734
1982	48,000	145,477
1983	50,000	180,660
1984	52,000	193,985
1985	54,000	257,916
1986	56,000	308,261
1987	58,000	326,394
1988	60,000	382,579
1989	62,000	501,260
1990	64,000	487,558
1991	66,000	644,210

Total value on 12/31/91 of $2,000 invested annually at 10 percent compounded rate without any up or down market fluctuations: $488,917.

The 33-year period represented in Figure 14.1 was one of widely fluctuating common stock prices in which there were years of both rapidly rising and falling markets. While there was never a time when the total value of the account was less than the total amount invested, it is certainly possible.

BEGINNING DOLLAR COST AVERAGING IN A DOWNTURN

If the plan in Figure 14.1 had been started in 1973, as stock prices were declining, the account would have shown a substantial loss at the end of both 1973 and 1974. In 1973 the market (as measured by the S&P 500 Index) dropped 14.7 percent and in 1974 it dropped 26.3 percent. At the end of 1973, with $2,000 invested, the account value would have been $1,706; and at the end of 1974, with $4,000 invested, the value would have been $2,731.

The investor who persevered, however, would have benefitted by buying more shares at the lower prices. In 1975 the market rebounded 37.1 percent, and in 1976 it went up by 23.8 percent. By the end of 1975, with $6,000 now invested, the investor would have had a value of $6,486. And at the end of 1976, with $8,000 invested, the account would have been worth $10,506.

During the four-year period 1973–76, the stock market dropped by a total of 41 percent in the first two years and then rose by a total of 60.9 percent in the last two years. Notice the effect of this volatility using 100 as a base:

$$
\begin{array}{llllll}
1973 & 100.0 & - & 14.7\% & = & 85.3 \\
1974 & 85.3 & - & 26.3\% & = & 59.0 \\
1975 & 59.0 & + & 37.1\% & = & 80.9 \\
1976 & 80.9 & + & 23.8\% & = & 100.1 \\
\end{array}
$$

Even though the two-year market recovery (60.9 percent) was substantially greater than the two-year loss (41 percent), it ended up at barely more than the original value of 100. This is because the recovery began from a much lower base.

Beginning a dollar cost averaging program at the start of what was a very severe stock market decline in 1973–74, and its subsequent recovery, worked out very much to the investor's advantage. With

$8,000 invested and a value of $10,506 at the end of 1976, the investor would have achieved a 31.3 percent return on his or her money.

SUMMARY

The widely used concept of dollar cost averaging helps to assure favorable long-term investment results. Fluctuating market conditions actually enhance the performance of such a systematic investment program. The benefits of dollar cost averaging depend on the assumption that the securities in which one invests will go up or down about as the general market does and sooner or later will rise in value. Persistence in continuing to buy shares regularly throughout periods of declining, as well as rising, prices is essential to produce the kind of results that have been illustrated.

CHAPTER 15

Special Opportunities

As we have already noted, long-term growth funds that are not restricted as to the types of securities they are permitted to buy generally have the best performance records over the long run. There are a number of reasons for this, not the least of which is the advantage of industry and geographical diversification.

For example, a particular industry can be hit by an unexpected downturn in business that is not the result of general economic conditions, or a regional recession can take place in one isolated area of the country. By having your investments diversified among many industries and in companies with different geographical areas of concentration, risk is reduced and there is less likelihood of missing out on major advances of the stock market. Nevertheless, there are times when particular industries will enjoy periods of strong growth in revenues and/or profits. If you can identify these swings and time your purchase of shares correctly, you can profit handsomely.

Everyone wants to buy at the bottom and sell at the top. Unfortunately, in the real world it doesn't often happen. Instead, observe when the downtrend of an industry's stock prices appears to have bottomed out and the general price movement has been somewhat lateral for a period of time. By waiting, you may miss some of the early profits in the subsequent upturn, but it will help avoid the risk that the downtrend has not yet found a bottom. Market timing is difficult, and success is often as much the result of luck as it is of analytical skill.

SPECIALIZED FUNDS

The investor who has special areas of interest or who wants to participate in the securities of a particular industry can choose from a number of specialty funds. The funds that specialize have investment policies designed to target the specific industries or geographical locations in which they concentrate their investments. In this chapter, we will examine a few funds that have performed well and have existed long enough to have at least five-year track records.

First, Figure 15.1 is a list of industries or geographical areas that are currently represented by mutual funds. Since there may be only one or just a few funds in each grouping, load funds are included in the list. The maximum sales charge is listed following each fund or fund group that charges a load.

The following is a listing which supplies brief descriptions of individual funds in each of several industry classifications that are popular with investors and have been in operation long enough to have five-year performance records. Although we have selected mutual funds with reasonably good records, the purpose is not to recommend these particular funds but rather to describe the objectives and policies of the funds, each of which represents a different industry group.

Energy

The Fidelity Select Energy portfolio, with over $80 million in assets, was first offered in December 1981. Its investment objective is growth of capital, and it focuses on companies that operate in energy and related industries. It recently was 87 percent invested in common stocks, with its largest holdings in Texaco, Phillips Petroleum, Kerr-McGee, Renaissance Energy, Amerada Hess, Elf Aquitaine, Hamilton Oil, Exxon and Mobil.

Total Return for Period Ending 12/31/91

1 Year	5 Years	Percent Yield Last 12 Months
0.0%	55.4%	1.0%

Source: CDA/Wiesenberger Investment Companies Service.

FIGURE 15.1 Specialized Funds by Category

Air Transportation
Fidelity Select Air Transportation (3%)

Automotive
Fidelity Select Automotive (3%)

Banks
Fidelity Select Regional Banks (3%)
Freedom Investment Trust I Regional Banks

Biotechnology
Fidelity Select Biotechnology (3%)
Oppenheimer Global Bio-Tech (5.75%)

Broadcast and Media
Fidelity Select Broadcast and Media (3%)

Brokerage and Investments
Fidelity Select Brokerage and Investments (3%)

Chemicals
Fidelity Select Chemicals (3%)

Computers
Fidelity Select Computers (3%)

Communications
Fidelity Select Developing Communications (3%)
Seligman Communications and Information (4.75%)

Construction and Housing
Fidelity Select Construction and Housing (3%)

Consumer Products
Fidelity Select Consumer Products (3%)

Defense and Aerospace
Fidelity Select Defense and Aerospace (3%)

Electronics
Fidelity Select Electronics (3%)

Energy
Fidelity Select Energy (3%)
Financial Strategic Energy
Neuberger Berman Selected Sectors
Putnam Energy Resources (8.5%)

Environmental Services
Fidelity Select Environmental Services (3%)

European
Financial Strategic European

FIGURE 15.1   Specialized Funds by Category (continued)

Financial Services
Century Shares Trust
Fidelity Select Financial Services (3%)
Financial Strategic Financial Services

Food and Agriculture
Fidelity Select Food and Agriculture (3%)

Gold/Precious Metals
Benham Gold Equities Index Fund
Blanchard Precious Metals Fund
Bull and Bear Gold Investors Limited
Fidelity Select American Gold (3%)
Fidelity Select Precious Metals and Minerals (3%)
Financial Strategic Gold
Keystone Precious Metals
Lexington Gold Fund
Oppenheimer Gold and Special Minerals (8.5%)
United Services Gold Shares
USAA Gold
Vanguard Specialized Gold and Precious Metals

Health Care
Fidelity Select Health Care (3%)
Financial Strategic Health Sciences
G.T. Global Health Care Fund (4.75%)
Medical Research Investment (4.75%)
Putnam Health Sciences Trust (5.75%)
Vanguard Specialized Health Care

Industrial Materials
Fidelity Select Industrial Materials (3%)

Information
Putnam Information Sciences (8.5%)

Insurance
Century Shares Trust
Fidelity Select Insurance (3%)

Leisure
Fidelity Select Leisure & Entertainment (3%)
Financial Strategic Leisure

Natural Resources
Merrill Lynch Natural Resources Trust B*

FIGURE 15.1   Specialized Funds by Category (continued)

Pacific Basin
Financial Strategic Pacific Basin
Nomura Pacific Basin Fund

Paper and Forest Products
Fidelity Select Paper and Forest Products (3%)

Retailing
Fidelity Select Retailing (3%)

Savings and Loan
Fidelity Select Savings and Loan (3%)

Science
United Science and Energy (8.5%)

Service Economy
Vanguard Specialized Service Economy

Software (Computers)
Fidelity Select Software and Computer (3%)

Technology
Fidelity Select Technology (3%)
Financial Strategic Technology

Telecommunications
Flag Telephone Income (3%)

Transportation
Fidelity Select Transportation (3%)

Utilities
ABT Utility Income Fund (4.75%)
Fidelity Select Utilities (3%)
Financial Strategic Utilities
Franklin Utilities (4%)
Stratton Monthly Dividend Shares

*Back-end Load.

Gold and Precious Metals

The Lexington Gold Fund, with some $93 million in assets, had its initial public offering in May 1979. Its objective is to attain capital appreciation through investment in gold and equity securities of companies engaged in the mining or processing of gold anywhere in the world.

The fund has been invested approximately 78 percent in common stocks of gold-mining companies, 19 percent in gold bullion and 3 percent in cash equivalents. Its largest holdings recently were American Barrick, Placer Dome, Homestake Mining, Rustenberg Platinum and Newmont Mining.

Total Return for Period Ending 12/31/91

1 Year	5 Years	Percent Yield Last 12 Months
–6.1%	14.4%	0.9%

Source: CDA/Wiesenberger Investment Companies Service.

Health Care

The Fidelity Select Health Care fund, first offered in July 1981, has $181 million in assets. Its objective is growth of capital, and it seeks to achieve this by investing in the health care industry. It recently had 98 percent of its assets committed to common stocks. The largest holdings were in Pfizer, Syntex, AMgen, American Cyanamid, Warner-Lambert, Bard, Bristol-Myers Squibb and Medco Containment Services.

Total Return for Period Ending 12/31/91

1 Year	5 Years	Percent Yield Last 12 Months
83.7%	251.7%	0.3%

Source: CDA/Wiesenberger Investment Companies Service.

Medical Delivery

The Fidelity Select Medical Delivery fund, with $134 million in assets, was first offered in 1986. Its objective is growth of capital with investments predominantly in companies engaged in the ownership or management of hospitals, nursing homes, health maintenance organizations and other companies specializing in the delivery of health care services.

This fund recently had 91 percent of its assets in common stocks and the balance in cash equivalents. Holdings were concentrated in five major areas: medical facilities management, medical equipment and supplies, real estate investment trusts, drugs and pharmaceuticals. Its largest holdings were in National Medical Enterprises, Humana, U.S. Healthcare, United Healthcare, Medical Care International and Community Psychiatric Centers.

Total Return for Period Ending 11/29/91

1 Year	5 Years	Percent Yield Last 12 Months
64.8%	165.4%	0.0%

Source: CDA/Wiesenberger Investment Companies Service.

Utilities

Stratton Monthly Dividend Shares was originally offered as a closed-end fund in 1972 and was listed on the American Stock Exchange. It became an open-end mutual fund in November 1981 and now has $38 million in assets. Its investment objective is to seek a high income return from common stocks and securities convertible into common stocks.

Approximately half of Stratton's funds are invested in electric and gas utilities, with the balance in industries such as real estate, savings and loans, energy and construction. The five largest individual stock holdings recently were Meditrust, DPL, Pennsylvania Power & Light, Washington Water Power and Central Hudson Gas & Electric.

Total Return for Period Ending 12/31/91

1 Year	5 Years	Percent Yield Last 12 Months
35.1%	50.0%	6.9%

Source: CDA/Wiesenberger Investment Companies Service.

ANOTHER SPECIAL OPPORTUNITY: TODAY'S SUPER CHECKING ACCOUNTS

At last you can get a competitive rate of interest on your checking account. It's safe and convenient, and you can arrange everything by mail without ever leaving your home. Today's mutual fund money market accounts provide all this and more.

Safety

The first concern of most people who open a money market account is likely to be an assurance that their money is safe. Rest easily. No major money market fund has ever defaulted.

Nonetheless, the first thing to do is to obtain and read the prospectus. A toll-free call to an 800 number will bring all the information you need to make an informed decision. The prospectus indicates the fund's holdings, typically U.S. Treasury securities and commercial paper, which is unsecured short-term corporate debt. See Appendix B for a listing of distributors, most of which have money market mutual funds.

Top-quality commercial paper, which is rated A-1 or A-2, has proven to be safe, but investors who are extremely conscious of risk might prefer funds that invest only in treasuries. That choice, however, probably will result in a somewhat lower yield.

Yield

Because of the short-term nature of investments held by money market funds (normally less than nine months), yields can change daily. The change will be slight, though, and is measured in *basis points.* (A basis point is one one-hundredth of 1 percent.) For example, if Fund A yields 4.82 percent and Fund B yields 4.95 percent, Fund B is said to be yielding 13 basis points more than Fund A. You will find substantial differences in yield among the more than 200 taxable money market funds and 90 or more tax-exempt funds.

In early March of 1992, investors who wanted a high yield could get 4.42 percent in the Dreyfus Worldwide Dollar Money Market Fund, which invests in dollar-denominated securities traded anywhere in the world. The average yield of all money market funds at that time was 3.85 percent. The yield figures are seven-day compound effective yields, which assumes that all income is reinvested. Major newspapers list money market funds and their yields once a week, making comparison shopping easy. For investors seeking a high tax-free income at that time, the Bayshore Tax-Free Fund was yielding 3.50 percent, while the average of all tax-exempt money market funds was 2.66 percent.

An important factor that affects the yield of money market funds is the *expense ratio* (the proportion that a fund's expenses bears to its total net assets). Look for funds with low expense ratios. They will generally produce higher returns. In early March 1992 the Keystone Liquid Trust, with an expense ratio of 1 percent, had a yield of 3.35 percent. On the other hand, the Vanguard Money Market Prime had a yield of 4.2 percent, with an expense ratio of only 0.28 percent. The difference of 0.72 percent in expenses was reflected in their yields.

Most money market funds permit check writing, which gives them a high degree of convenience and usefulness. The prospectus will tell you about such things as costs and limitations on writing checks. Many funds permit checks to be written only in minimum amounts, such as $100, $250 or $500. They may or may not assess any charges.

Fidelity's high-yielding Spartan Money fund charges $2 for each check written. In contrast, Fidelity Cash Reserves offers free check writing but imposes a $500 minimum on each check. Other funds allow unlimited check writing, with no minimum-size checks and no charges per transaction, but they may charge annual fees.

Other Considerations

Other factors to consider include the minimum investment required and whether a fund is part of a family of funds. Some money market funds have minimum initial purchase amounts as low as $250 (Financial Daily Income Shares), and others may go as high as $20,000 (Fidelity Spartan Money). Most funds have minimum initial investments in the $1,000 to $2,500 range. Additional deposits into a fund are normally permitted in minimum amounts as low as $50.

If a money market fund is part of a fund family, it allows for easy switching into equity or bond funds. This gives an investor the flexibility to move his or her money in or out of the stock or bond markets quickly and conveniently. This usually can be handled by a phone call and will be done as of the close of the market on the same day. Most mutual funds charge $5 for the switching service.

SUMMARY

Growth funds with unrestricted investment policies have generally outperformed specialized funds over the long pull. Specialty funds, however, can have sharp increases in value at certain times. Two examples of this include the dramatic rise in gold shares a decade ago and more recently, the rapid increase in the prices of health care and medical delivery shares. The investor who wants to participate in a particular industry or geographical area can often find a fund that concentrates its holdings in his or her field of interest.

Money market funds provide a safe and profitable haven for your funds. They can be used as super checking accounts or simply as places to park money while you await attractive investment opportunities.

CHAPTER 16

How Greed Can Cost You Money

Greed is a harsh word. We don't usually think of ourselves as being greedy—other people are greedy. The *Random House Dictionary of the English Language* defines greed as "the desire for something, often more than one's proper share." It is in that sense that the investor is often hurt, generally by a loss of capital.

In the purchase and ownership of mutual funds, there basically are three parties whose greed can be responsible for your losing money: (1) you, (2) your broker and (3) mutual fund companies.

THE INVESTOR'S GREED

All too often the old saw "I saw the enemy and it was I!" is true. In the final analysis, we can sometimes be our own worst enemies. When we strive for more than our "proper share," trouble cannot be far off. We seek yields that are too high and capital gains that come too quickly and are too high—and we love to get something for nothing.

For the mutual fund investor, there are several types of offerings that should be investigated carefully before buying. They are as follows:

- High-yield bond funds, especially "enhanced" U.S. government bond funds
- Option income funds
- The current "hot" growth fund
- Funds with no front-end loads, but with early redemption charges

- Whenever your broker recommends switching out of one family of funds into another
- New offerings of closed-end funds

How Much Yield Can You Expect?

There are rarely any free lunches in the financial markets. On March 2, 1992, *Barron's,* the weekly business magazine, reported the following yields on various securities:

1-year Treasury bills	4.21%
10-year Treasury bonds	7.31
30-year 8.50% GNMAs	8.13
High-grade corporate bonds	8.23
Medium-grade corporate bonds	8.85
High-yield (low-grade) bonds	14.47
Municipal bond index	6.74
50 stock dividend yields	2.98

Normally, the higher the yield is, the greater the risk. U.S. government-backed securities will yield less than corporate issues, and short-term Treasury bills usually will pay less than long-term government bonds.

In corporate bonds, the higher the quality is, the lower the yield. Municipal bonds, of course, always pay less because they are tax-exempt. Dividends on common stocks generally are low because corporations want to reinvest most of their earnings back into their businesses to finance future growth.

Using these standards as a guide, if the yield on a mutual fund you are considering is significantly higher than the current rates on the type of securities it holds, be wary. Remember, too, that the fund deducts all its expenses from the income it collects before making its dividend payout to the investor. Thus, because of expenses, the high yield you are being offered is actually substantially less than what the fund must earn on its portfolio to make the payment.

High-Yield Bond Funds

Let's assume that a fund owns a portfolio of lower-grade bonds with an average yield of 13.63 percent. Its expense ratio (expenses as a percentage of assets) is 0.89 percent. After subtracting the expense ratio from the average yield, the dividend distribution rate is 12.74 percent. That is realistic, based on market conditions at the time, but this is not to say that it is a safe investment. High-yield bonds imply a fairly high degree of risk.

Now along comes another fund with a 13.5 percent dividend distribution rate. Be careful of this fund. How can they do it? Here are three ways, but note that two of them can hurt you:

1. The bonds in the fund are of even lower quality, thereby increasing the yield but also increasing *your* risk that they will default. (It happens!)
2. The manager is trading securities in the fund to produce short-term capital gains, which are then paid out as capital distributions. Again, this is an increase in risk, and it often results in a gradual decline over time in net asset value (NAV).
3. It's a new fund trying to capture market share, and management temporarily waives all or a portion of the expenses of running the fund. On this basis, they can pay out a greater amount of the income collected from the bonds in the fund, at least until they decide to start charging the full expenses. Until then, it's a winner for you—at no extra risk.

High-Yield U.S. Government Bond Funds

An investment in one of these funds can cause you to lose money and sleep. These funds sound good because they hold only securities guaranteed as to both principal and interest payments by the U.S. government or its agencies.

In early 1992 some of these funds were paying dividends at rates from 9.94 percent to as much as 10.28 percent. Keep in mind that U.S. government securities were paying 7.31 percent to 8.13 percent at the time. With expenses that can run over 1 percent, the funds must earn 10.94 percent to 11.28 percent to effect those payouts. How can they do that? First, they trade in the futures markets and sell options to make short-term capital gains. Second, they buy securities at a premium over their par value in order to get a higher current yield. But the value of the securities will eventually go back down to par when they mature, resulting in a capital loss to the fund.

This very risky business has resulted in the loss of principal to thousands of shareowners. They have seen the value of their investments decline so much over the years that even after taking into account the dividends they have received (and paid taxes on), they end up with less money than when they started. And this is with a "safe" investment—or so they were told.

Option Income Funds

This is another group of high-yielding funds to stay away from. Option income funds normally invest in common stocks and hold out very high dividend payouts as bait. One such fund, which is not the exception, was paying out more than 14 percent in early 1989. The only problem is that over the previous ten years, the fund's NAV per share had dropped by half. Many people bought these funds for the income payout, only to see their principal gradually disappear.

Where does the high payout come from? It certainly isn't just from stock dividends, which average about 3 percent. Instead, it mostly comes from the sale of options on stock held in the portfolio. The fund collects fees by selling options, giving other investors the right to buy stock at a specified price for a limited period of time. If the price of the stock goes up, the option will be exercised and the stock is called away (bought). If the price stays the same or goes down, the option is not exercised, and the fund keeps the stock. This means that if the stock market goes up, the fund doesn't benefit from the price rise because it loses the stock it sold options on and has to replace it with other stock at higher prices. In effect, there is a ceiling that keeps the fund's own shares from rising in value during a bull market, but there is no floor to keep them from falling when the stock market goes down. All in all, it's a very unhappy situation. In return for a high dividend payout, the investor watches the value of his or her principal sink.

Buying the Hot Growth Fund

For the investor seeking maximum capital appreciation, there is a temptation to buy today's hot fund. This is the fund touted as having had the best growth record for the last quarter or year. But be careful: it might not last.

Studies have shown that a fund whose performance is in the top 10 percent of all funds during a particular period will frequently wind up in the bottom 10 percent a year later. If you want to make money over the long run without running an inordinate amount of risk, buy into funds that demonstrate outstanding performance over an extended period of years. Look at a fund's one-, five- and ten-year records. The hot fund today may be cold tomorrow. Figure 16.1 shows the top-performing no-load mutual funds for the one-, five- and ten-year periods ending December 31, 1991.

Why do some funds have such explosive growth for a short period of time? One reason is luck. Another is that particularly in the smaller funds, they may hold relatively few stocks in their portfolios. If one or two stocks suddenly surge ahead, it will have a big impact on the fund. In a large fund with many stocks, a big price move by one or two stocks will have much less effect. The same is true on the downside, which sometimes explains why a hot fund suddenly turns cold. Sharp price

FIGURE 16.1   Top-Performing No-Load Mutual Funds

For the 12 Months Ending 12/31/91

CGM Capital Development Fund	99.2%
Financial Strategic Health Sciences	91.7
Berger 100 Fund	88.8
Twentieth Century Ultra Investors	86.4
Twentieth Century Giftrust Investors	84.6
Kaufmann Fund	79.5

For the 5 Years Ending 12/31/91

Financial Strategic Health Sciences	378.0%
Twentieth Century Ultra Investors	237.5
Berger 100 Fund	211.0
Vanguard Specialized Health Care	190.2
Twentieth Century Giftrust Investors	177.9
CGM Capital Development Fund	175.2

For the 10 Years Ending 12/31/91

CGM Capital Development Fund	882.0%
Financial Industrial Income Fund	525.6
Twentieth Century Ultra Investors	523.3
IAI Regional Fund	497.9
Sequoia Fund	489.5
Stein Roe Special Fund	486.5

Source: CDA/Wiesenberger Investment Companies Service.

drops by one or two issues will have a dramatic effect on the NAVs of small funds.

A second reason for a fund to turn in a spectacular performance may be that it is young. A new fund has flexibility. It is not held back by a lot of slow-moving stocks that have been accumulated over the years. The young, growing mutual fund can take advantage of bargains and can also load up with smaller, emerging-growth issues. In contrast, the giant funds have to buy large capitalization companies. Because of the huge amounts of cash they have to invest, they buy big blocks of stock. Their purchases of a small company's stock would immediately drive the price up, and conversely, when they sell, the price could be destroyed.

THE BROKER'S GREED

Never forget that a broker is paid on commission. He or she may be called an account executive, a financial consultant or some other euphemism, but the bottom line is that the broker is a salesperson. He or she gets paid only when you buy.

The problem with this is that the broker is faced with a dilemma in that he or she has a conflict of interests. The investor wants the broker's advice on what to do. The broker really wants to work in the customer's best interests, but he or she has to feed the family, buy gasoline for the Mercedes and pay for a host of other odds and ends. Therefore, there are certain things a broker will not do, and there are also things that a broker will do that perhaps he or she should not.

Back-End Load Funds

One thing your broker will not do is recommend that you invest in a no-load mutual fund. This only makes sense. There is no way that he or she can get paid if you go directly to a mutual fund and invest in a fund that has no sales charges.

However, your broker may recommend that you invest in a mutual fund that has no load (commission) when you buy but that will have a withdrawal charge if you pull out before a predetermined number of years, usually five or six. He or she may make it sound as if you are not paying any commission (but you are). When you buy, the broker gets paid immediately, usually 5 percent of the amount of your invest-ment. That has to come from somewhere, and it does. It comes right out of your pocket. An annual distribution charge of up to 1.25 percent is deducted each year from your invested assets in addition to the normal fund expense charges.

Churning

This sometimes happens when a broker needs business. It is illegal but very difficult to prove. *Churning* is selling a customer out of one investment and into another, when it isn't in the customer's best interests, in order to earn a commission.

Churning is dangerous and costs the investor money, not only in commissions paid but often in loss of capital. (The new investment may turn out to be worse than the one being sold.) Churning is also more commonplace than you might expect. Even the broker may have a guilty conscience after he or she churns a customer's account; but the broker is under great pressure to produce business and may be con-vinced that he or she is making a good recommendation. So when a broker suggests moving from one mutual fund into another (in a different fund group), he or she will offer some kind of reason to back it up. If the customer buys, the broker has earned another commission, and the investor is out some more money.

A conscientious broker will first determine whether a well-managed fund of the type he or she is recommending might be available within the same family of funds the investor is already in. If that is the case, an exchange can be made at no cost to the investor (except for a possible small transfer fee).

Closed-End-Fund New Issues

Another potentially poor investment to watch out for is the new issue of shares in a closed-end mutual fund. Such shares are sold to the public by mutual fund companies through broker-dealers and have become very popular in the last few years. Nothing is wrong with the closed-end fund in concept. Once the underwriting has been completed (all the shares have been sold), the shares are then listed for trading on a major stock exchange, usually the New York Stock Exchange.

The problem is that shortly after closed-end fund shares are listed for trading, they usually drop substantially in value from the original offering price. This occurs for two reasons. First, once the initial sales effort is over, there is very little demand from the public to support the market price. And second, the NAV per share of the closed-end fund is about 8 percent below the original offering price. That difference was paid out to the various parties involved in underwriting the new issue.

Unfortunately, when the customer was called and sold on the merits of the new closed-end fund, he or she may not have been told very forcefully that the shares would have a NAV of only about 92 percent of what he or she paid for them. Again, the need to earn commissions puts a great deal of pressure on the broker who is selling these new issues. In most cases, the investor would only have to wait two or three months to buy the shares on the New York Stock Exchange at a substantial discount from the offering price.

THE MUTUAL FUND'S GREED

Finally, the investor can be hurt because of the pressure on mutual fund companies to keep offering new products. Growth for a mutual fund company can come from three sources:

1. Increasing the value of its shares through market appreciation
2. New money being added to the funds from reinvested dividends and additional share purchases from investors
3. The establishment and sale of new funds

It is the establishment of new funds that can sometimes cause the investor grief. A fund may simply offer a new fund that it believes will have sales appeal.

The closed-end mutual fund is an example of a product that has had great sales appeal in recent years, even though many people have been burned by such funds. The appeal comes first from the fact that the investor buys shares at the offering price. He or she probably thinks there is no commission, since nothing is tacked on to what the investor pays. Next, there is the appeal of something new: The investor is "getting in on the ground floor." And finally, there is the sales pitch that extols all the benefits.

Another temptation for mutual fund companies is to find some exotic new type of fund that will appeal to investors. There have been quite a few of these, such as market-timing funds, special-industry-group funds, geographically oriented funds and so on. Many of them have not worked out nearly as well as the bread-and-butter funds that give management the flexibility to seek out the best investments, wherever they may be.

SUMMARY

In the end, the investor must always use prudence and common sense. He or she should not be led astray by greed—his or her own or that of anyone else.

PART THREE

Mutual Fund Strategies

C H A P T E R   1 7

How To Guarantee You'll Make Money

Everyone wants to find a "sure thing," a way to make money without any risk of losing your investment. Does it exist? A lot of people say no. They've tried every way they know and still always seem to end up "behind the eight ball." Then there are others who will assure you that they have a surefire investment that can't lose. They're like the penny-stock salesperson who calls at home when you're in the middle of dinner and says, "Have I got a deal for you!"

But there actually is a simple investment package you can easily put together yourself that will make you money while guaranteeing a return of your original investment. The only stipulation required to assure it will work is that you hold on to the investment for the time you originally set up.

THE ZERO-COUPON BOND/COMMON STOCK COMBINATION

The concept is easy. You make your investment in two parts: One portion goes into a zero-coupon U.S. government bond fund with a specific maturity date, and the balance goes into a growth fund with a good record of past performance. Choose any growth fund you like. To be sure the plan will work, hold the bond fund to maturity. At that time, you will receive your original investment back from the zero-coupon fund, and you will have the value of the growth fund. The growth fund would have to become worthless for you not to make a profit. Even then, you would still get back your original investment.

First, a zero-coupon U.S. government bond is one in which the right to its interest payments has been stripped away. The bond can then be bought by an investor at a substantial discount. Someone else buys the right to receive the interest payments. The stripped bond will eventually mature for its full face amount on the maturity date.

HOW THE PLAN WORKS

Let's assume that you have $10,000 to invest and can leave it untouched for a certain number of years. You can set the plan up for any number of years, selecting a bond fund that will mature on the date you desire. In this case, assume the plan has a maturity date in the year 2000.

Step 1

Invest a portion of your money in a zero-coupon U.S. government bond fund. The Scudder Group has one that matures in the third week of December of the year 2000. On March 6, 1992, based on the net asset value (NAV) of the fund that day, an investment of $1,000 will mature at that time for $1,691, in a little less than eight years.

To be assured of having $10,000 at that time, divide $10,000 by 1.691. This gives you $5,914, the amount to be invested in the zero-coupon fund, which will then mature for $10,000 in the third week of December 2000. (All amounts have been rounded to the nearest dollar.)

Step 2

Then invest the balance of the $10,000 in a growth fund. This amounts to $4,086. For the sake of this example, let's invest it in the Scudder Capital Growth Fund. You can't predict what this fund will do in the future; it could be worth more or less than the original investment. However, you can look back and see how the fund performed in the past. For the eight-year period ending September 30, 1991, the Scudder Capital Growth Fund had a total return of 160.47 percent. This is the approximate percent change in net assets per share with capital gains and income dividends reinvested. Thus, if we had invested $4,086 in the Scudder Capital Growth Fund on October 1, 1983, it would have been worth a total of $10,643 on September 30, 1991. Adding $10,643 to the $10,000 matured value of the zero-coupon fund produces a total value of $20,643. Keep in mind that past performance is not necessarily an indication of future results.

The U.S. government has always honored its obligations, and you can feel pretty confident that the zero-coupon bonds will be paid as promised at maturity. In the third week of December 2000, your zero-coupon bond fund will mature for $10,000. It must be stated that while the U.S. government stands behind the bonds it issues, it does not guarantee the shares of a mutual fund that holds them. To remove even that small element of risk, it is necessary to buy the zero-coupon bond itself (which can be done through a stock broker).

The Payoff

In summary, here is how your investment would look.

$10,000 Assumed Investment

	Zero-Coupon U.S. Government Bond Fund[1]	Scudder Capital Growth Fund[2]
Initial investment	$5,914	$4,086
Ending value	10,000	10,643

[1]Invested for eight years and nine months, from 3/6/92 to the third week of December 2000.
[2]A hypothetical eight-year investment ending on 9/30/91, with capital gains and income dividends reinvested. Not guaranteed.

This is my "sleep-well" investment. No matter what happens to the stock market, your original $10,000 will be safely returned at maturity. Remember, though, that if you need your money early, the zero-coupon government bond fund may be worth more or less than $10,000. Due to market conditions, even government bonds fluctuate in value prior to maturity.

TAX CONSIDERATIONS

As we noted earlier, zero-coupon bonds do not make interest payments to the holder. Instead, they are purchased at a substantial discount and then mature for the face amount of the bond. For tax purposes, however, the holder is considered to receive the interest each year on an imputed basis. Simply stated, you will be taxed annually on the interest even though you don't receive it. For this reason, many taxpayers hold zero-coupon bonds in their IRAs, KEOGH plans or other qualified retirement plans in which taxes are deferred.

SUMMARY

The zero-coupon bond/common stock combination enables the cautious investor to set up a plan that assures the return of his or her original investment while providing the opportunity for a substantial capital gain. The investor need only maintain the investment for the time originally stipulated. The approach is particularly attractive in a retirement plan that shields the investor from taxes until the program has been completed.

CHAPTER 18

How To Turn Your Losers into Winners in Ten Minutes

The toughest thing for any investor to face up to is having made a bad investment. No one likes to admit a mistake. And it doesn't help to blame a loser on someone else: a broker, a friend, a brother, a tip, etc. There it sits. What are you going to do? In less than ten minutes, you can turn your loser into a winner.

By the way, nothing improves your mental attitude about your investments more than dumping a dog you've held onto for too long. The old axiom "out of sight, out of mind" definitely applies to the bad investments you dump. As long as you continue to own a loser, it will continue to nag at you and keep you unsettled, unhappy and maybe even awake at night. But once you're out of it, it's gone. Before you know it "the old is passed away," and your new, profitable investment will have you content and sleeping again.

GET OUT OF THE FRYING PAN—NOW!

The first step to take with a poorly performing mutual fund investment is to flee to safety. Pick up the telephone and call your fund's toll-free 800 number. Ask for the investor services department and instruct them to move all shares of the fund into their money market fund. They will take care of it immediately, and you will be credited with the net asset value (NAV) of your fund as of 4:00 P.M. on the day you called. Most mutual funds are part of a family of funds that will include at least one money market fund.

Having done this, you already will have turned your loser into a winner. How?

1. It gets you out of a bad situation that might have gotten worse. I have seen situations where the share value of a fund has gone down substantially, and it seems there can't be any more downside risk. But there is: it just keeps going down.
2. You now have time to breathe. There's no longer any pressure on you to *do* something. You can relax and coolly consider what you might want to do next in terms of longer-term investment planning.
3. Your money is safe. It won't fluctuate in value. You won't be looking at the newspaper every day wondering how much you lost.
4. Best of all, you know you've invested in a winner. Your money is now earning a positive and good rate of return, with interest dividends compounding monthly.

There is frequently a $5 administrative fee for moving assets from one fund to another within the same family, and it's worth it. On the other hand, a few funds make no charge at all, which makes sense. After all, you can move assets from one no-load mutual fund group to another no-load group without incurring any cost. However, there might be a few days of earnings lost in making a transfer from one fund group to another.

Your fund may require the telephone exchange privilege to be set up ahead of time in order to use it. If so, get that done as quickly as possible. You never know when you might want to make use of it. It's a very convenient service and provides you with a great deal of control and flexibility in your investing. If your fund does not permit telephone exchanges, move your money to one that does!

BUT BEFORE YOU JUMP . . .

You're now out of a loser and into a winner, with your money safe and earning a good return. But you may be looking for something else with more potential for the long term. One thing you don't want is to move into another loser.

First, take another careful look at the fund you just left. Why did you buy it in the first place? Was your reasoning valid? Perhaps only the timing was off. You might want to consider the performance of other funds of the same type during the time you were in the losing fund. If all such funds did poorly, maybe funds with this investment objective and management policy are about to participate in the next upside of their investment cycle. You might even consider eventually returning to the fund. But if the group did well and your fund was one of the few that didn't, there probably is a management problem, and you're better off leaving the fund.

The second step is to return to square one and review your investment objectives. Once you're back on the right track from the standpoint of knowing the type of fund that meets your objectives, select a fund that has a proven record of good past performance. Use a mutual fund service that you subscribe to or can access at your local public library for the facts and guidance that can help you make a sound decision.

SUMMARY

Remember that when you make an exchange from one fund to another, even if both funds are in the same group, a taxable event occurs. Coming out of a fund at a price below what you paid for it creates a tax loss, which you can use to offset against taxable income up to $3,000 in one year. (Any balance can be carried forward to offset against future income.) Or, you can use the loss against capital gains you may have realized. Similarly, exchanging from shares in which you have a profit will produce a capital gain. See Chapter 23 ("How To Calculate Taxable Gains and Losses").

CHAPTER 19

Timing Your Purchases To Avoid Taxes

Investors sometimes try to capture an extra income or capital gains distribution by purchasing mutual fund shares just before an expected payout is to be made. This is usually a mistake.

Mutual funds generally pay income and capital gains distributions at predetermined times—monthly, quarterly or annually. There is a temptation to buy shares just before a distribution is made in order to increase total return. In the case of capital gains and usually for income dividends, however, the net asset value (NAV) of a share will drop by the exact amount of the distribution on the day it is made. Thus, the investor is even; he or she has no gain. What the investor does have, though, is a tax liability based on the amount of the distribution. Payment of an income or capital gains distribution is a taxable event and will cost the investor money. This problem can easily be avoided by waiting until the day after the distribution is effective to make a purchase.

The tax penalty for making this mistake can be most severe with equity funds, where large capital gains are often distributed just before or after December 31st. In a strong stock market, where a fund has realized substantial capital gains on stocks it has sold, it may pay a capital gain of as much as 20 percent of the share value. The share price will then drop by that amount. An investor who purchased shares shortly before the distribution will be faced with a substantial income tax bill, but he or she has enjoyed no gain in value whatsoever.

Even on bond funds, where income dividends ordinarily are paid monthly, find out when the next dividend is to be paid and then make a judgment as to whether it is better to invest now or wait until after the distribution is made.

Keep these two factors in mind:

1. Other things being equal, share prices tend to move up as a dividend payment date approaches.
2. After a dividend is paid and the share price drops, you can buy more shares for the same dollar investment. This will result in greater future dividends on the shares you own.

Example:

Stockholders of record in the Value Line Leveraged Growth Investors fund on December 17, 1991, received a dividend of $.23 and a capital gains distribution of $4.61 per share, which were paid on December 23. The following illustration indicates the effect of purchasing shares of the fund on December 17 or of waiting until December 18. A slight decline in the stock market on December 18 caused the NAV to decline by $4.90, $.06 more than the combined amount of the dividend and capital gains distribution.

Assumed Investment of $10,000

Purchase Date	NAV	Shares Purchased	Distribution Received
12/17/91	$28.19	354.73	$1,716.89
12/18/91	23.29	429.36	0.00

An investor who invested $10,000 in the Value Line Leveraged Growth Investors fund on December 17 would have received 354.73 shares at a cost of $28.19 per share. He or she then received a dividend and capital gains distribution of $1,716.92 ($4.84 × 354.73 shares). On December 18, the share price dropped by the amount of the distribution (plus $.06) to $23.29, and the shares then had a total value of $8,261.66 ($23.29 × 354.73). The investor also had the $1,716.92 distribution, for an approximate total value of $9,978.58. (The total also reflects a small decrease due to the stock market decline on December 18.) The problem is that the investor must report a dividend and capital gain totaling $1,716.94 to the IRS. This would result in paying taxes of $532.25 for a person in the 31 percent tax bracket.

The investor who bought this fund on December 18 was not entitled to the dividend or capital gains distribution but bought 429.36 shares at $23.29 per share with a total value of $10,000. Both investors ended up with approximately the same asset value, but the one who waited a day to invest had no tax liability.

Warning:

There is always risk. In this case, the stock market went down on December 18, 1991, and an investor was able to buy more shares on that date. The reverse would be true if the stock market had advanced. However, a stock market increase would have had to have been quite significant for it to have impacted the investor adversely, taking taxes into consideration.

SUMMARY

To avoid paying income taxes on a taxable event that may be no benefit to you, time your purchases of mutual fund shares carefully. Try not to buy into a fund shortly before a dividend or capital gains distribution is to be paid. Most funds make distributions just before or just after December 31. Some pay dividends on a quarterly or even monthly basis.

CHAPTER 20

How To Defer Income Taxes for Years and Years

The government-sponsored *individual retirement account (IRA)* is one of the best tax-advantaged ways to supplement your retirement income. All wage earners under the age of $70\frac{1}{2}$ are permitted to set up IRAs. Most mutual funds offer IRA plans to eligible investors. They are both simple and economical to arrange and to maintain.

Three components make up an individual's prudent retirement program: (1) Social Security as a foundation; (2) income from your own savings, investments or employer retirement plan; and (3) an IRA.

The magic of an IRA lies in the tax benefits that permit an eligible wage earner to make tax-deductible contributions that then compound on a tax-deferred basis. This makes it possible to build up a significantly bigger retirement fund than would otherwise be possible where income and realized capital gains are taxed each year. It also removes the constraints on investment decisions that arise from tax considerations. There is no concern about whether or not to sell an investment on which there is a substantial capital gain, since there is no current tax liability.

STRATEGIES OF IRA INVESTING

Two aspects of an IRA have an important bearing on how you plan your investment strategy. First, the purpose of an IRA is to develop a retirement income. Second, all income dividends and capital gains distributions accumulate tax-deferred. Since there is a more or less

127

fixed time in the future when you will want to use your retirement funds, it makes sense to map out now a sound investment program that you can put into effect and stick with.

A faithfully maintained IRA, with regular annual contributions, is the almost ideal example of dollar cost averaging. (See Chapter 14, "Using the All-Time Favorite Investment Technique.") The younger you are when you start an IRA, the better it works. An investor who contributes $2,000 a year to an IRA for 30 years—say, beginning at age 35—and whose funds compound at 10 percent per year, will accumulate the sum of $361,884 at age 65.

For IRA participants who intend to retire more than ten years in the future, I recommend investing in one or more growth funds. This is because every study made of long-term investing concludes that equity mutual funds consistently outperform those that hold debt securities. Select a fund, or funds, that have at least a ten-year record of solid performance.

When you are within five years of retirement, consider moving at least some of your assets into fixed-income funds. During that five-year period, there probably will be a time when the stock market is relatively high. That is the time to move funds to a safe haven—even into a money market fund. It is no fun to be caught in a bear market just when you want to retire and watch the value of your IRA portfolio take a nose dive.

The second aspect of an IRA that is important to you as an investor is the fact that there are no current taxes to pay as your funds accumulate. This means that you need take no special investment actions that are based solely on tax considerations. It leaves you free to choose the best-performing investments, regardless of whether they generate high current income or capital gain distributions.

ELIGIBILITY

If neither you nor your spouse is an active participant in a retirement plan, you may make a contribution of up to the lesser of $2,000 (or $2,250 in the case of a spousal IRA), or 100 percent of compensation, and take a tax deduction for the entire amount contributed.

If you are an active participant in a retirement plan but have an adjusted gross income below a certain level (see the next section, "The

Deductibility of Contributions"), you may make a deductible contribution. If, however, you or your spouse is an active participant and your combined adjusted gross income is above the specified level, the amount of the deductible contribution you may make to an IRA is phased down and eventually eliminated.

THE DEDUCTIBILITY OF CONTRIBUTIONS

The deductibility of your annual contribution depends upon whether you are covered by another retirement plan and the amount of your adjusted gross income.

Your contribution is fully deductible:

- If you are not covered by another retirement plan, regardless of your adjusted gross income, up to $2,000
- If you are covered by another retirement plan but your adjusted gross income is less than $25,050
- If you are married and file a joint return, even though you are covered by another retirement plan, as long as your combined adjusted gross income is less than $40,050
- If you are a married taxpayer filing a separate return and are not personally covered by a retirement plan, regardless of adjusted gross income

Your contribution is partially deductible:

- If you are covered by another retirement plan and your adjusted gross income is between $25,050 and $34,999 (single). You may contribute from $200 to $1,990.
- If you are married, file a joint return, are covered by another retirement plan and your combined adjusted gross income is between $40,050 and $49,999. You may contribute from $200 to $1,990 each.
- If you are married, file a separate return, are covered by another retirement plan and have an adjusted gross income of less than $10,000.
- Minimum IRA deduction allowed: $200.

Your contribution is not deductible:

- If you are single, are covered by another retirement plan and your adjusted gross income is over $35,000. You can make a tax-deferred, but nondeductible, $2,000 investment.
- If you are married and file a joint return, are covered by another retirement plan and have a combined adjusted gross income over $50,000. You and your spouse can make tax-deferred, but nondeductible, $2,000 investments.
- If you are married and file a separate return, are covered by another retirement plan and have an adjusted gross income of $10,000 or more. You can make a tax-deferred, but nondeductible, $2,000 investment.

NONDEDUCTIBLE CONTRIBUTIONS

You can make nondeductible contributions to your IRA. Of course, your total contribution for the year cannot exceed the maximum amount allowable (the lesser of 100 percent of compensation or $2,000). Regardless of whether the contribution is deductible or nondeductible, IRA earnings still compound on a tax-deferred basis.

SPOUSAL IRAs

You can contribute to a spousal IRA even if your spouse has earned some compensation during the year. Provided your spouse does not make a contribution to an IRA, you can set up a spousal IRA consisting of an account for your spouse as well as an account for yourself. The maximum deductible amount for a spousal IRA is the lesser of $2,250 or 100 percent of compensation.

ROLLOVER IRAs

One of the most important provisions of the IRA is the *rollover* contribution. This permits the deposit into an IRA of a distribution from a qualified pension or profit-sharing plan. Such funds may later be transferred back to a qualified pension or profit-sharing plan, subject to acceptance under the plan and approval of the new employer. There is no tax liability when moving funds from a qualified plan to an IRA or back again.

To receive favorable tax treatment, a rollover contribution must meet the following requirements:

- It must result from separation from the service of the employer.
- It must be the full distribution from the plan. Or, if a partial distribution, it must be at least 50 percent of the total amount owed or must result from disability while employed (or death of your spouse while he or she was under the plan and you are the beneficiary).
- It must be deposited in an IRA within 60 days of the date of the distribution.

DISTRIBUTIONS FROM AN IRA

Since IRAs were developed to allow individuals to build funds for retirement, there are substantial penalties for premature withdrawals. Penalties apply only to contributions on which tax deductions were taken and to tax-sheltered earnings. There is no penalty on funds taken out that relate to nondeductible contributions.

In general, distributions may not begin prior to age $59\frac{1}{2}$ and must begin by age $70\frac{1}{2}$. Partial or total distributions can be taken when the participant reaches age $59\frac{1}{2}$. Such amounts may be a portion or all of the funds in the account. When a participant reaches age $70\frac{1}{2}$, however, either the total amount in the account must be taken or a regular income must begin, payable over a period certainly not extending beyond the life expectancy of the participant or of the participant and his or her beneficiary.

All distributions from tax-sheltered contributions and earnings will be taxed as ordinary income, whether taken before or after age $59\frac{1}{2}$. However, there is also a 10 percent excise tax penalty on any amounts withdrawn from an IRA prior to age $59\frac{1}{2}$, with one important exception. If the money is withdrawn based on a life expectancy table, the penalty is waived.

SUMMARY

Mutual-fund-sponsored IRAs represent an excellent vehicle for building retirement funds on a highly tax-favored basis. While not all wage earners qualify for tax-deductible contributions, nearly all can take advantage of the tax-deferred accumulation privilege.

A 35-year-old wage earner, contributing just $2,000 a year for 30 years and compounding his or her account at 10 percent annually, will retire at age 65 with an IRA fund worth $361,884.

CHAPTER 21

How To Avoid the Cost and Delay of Probate

Most of us are long-term investors, and someday we'll depart this world for a better place. Since we won't be taking our mutual funds along with us, let's look at a simple and inexpensive way to make sure these assets go to whom we want in the quickest and most efficient way.

Most individuals own mutual funds in their own names or with someone else as joint tenant. These are very satisfactory ways to own funds as long as we're alive, but what happens at death? In the case of an individual, if he or she has a will, the mutual funds will be disposed of under the terms of the will. If there is no will, the state having jurisdiction will write a will for that person, meaning that the funds will be distributed in accordance with the laws of the state in which he or she lived.

When mutual funds are owned as joint tenants with rights of survivorship and one of the joint tenants dies, ownership can quite easily be transferred to the survivor(s). In most cases, all that is required to effect the transfer is a certified copy of the death certificate and an affidavit of domicile. The process is speedy and simple. (Incidentally, the question of whether it is appropriate for you to hold mutual funds—and other assets—as joint tenants should be discussed with your attorney. The tax and estate-planning considerations are too important to be left to chance.)

THE PROBATE COURT

In any event, unless you take specific action to avoid it, your mutual fund assets will eventually end up in probate court. This is because in every part of the United States there exists a special court that is involved with the administration of estates. Most commonly called probate court, it is also referred to as the orphans, surrogate or chancery court.

Your *executor,* as named in your will (or appointed by the court if you die intestate—without a will), has the duty to present your will to the probate court with an inventory of the assets and liabilities of your estate. The court will determine the legality of the will and accept it for probate. A legal notice will be inserted in a local newspaper, notifying your creditors of your death and giving them an opportunity to present their claims. The court will hear any claims of interested parties against the estate and will take care of other matters that properly come under its jurisdiction.

There are three unhappy consequences of having your mutual funds and other assets probated under the jurisdiction of the court:

1. **Probating is time-consuming.** In a survey of knowledgeable attorneys across the country, the time required to probate a will was indicated to be from two to five years!
2. **Probating attracts publicity.** Private matters can become newspaper headlines. Local reporters always cover the probate court. Also, from probate court records, lists of widows are compiled and sold to people who prey on beneficiaries to separate them from their money.
3. **Probating is costly.** The cost of estate administration can be exceedingly high. In the case of small estates ($10,000 to $20,000), it can average 20 percent. On medium-sized estates in the $100,000 range, it runs about 10 percent. For larger estates, the percentages will be smaller, but the amounts can be very large.

It can be very much to your advantage to avoid the time, cost and publicity involved in the probate process—and there is an easy way to do it.

THE LIVING TRUST

The way to become immune to the probate process is through use of the *inter vivos* or *living trust,* a financial bridge from one generation to another. The term *inter vivos* means something that takes place during the lifetime of the persons involved. Thus, it is commonly referred to as a living trust. It is simply a document that you set up while you are alive and that goes into immediate operation. The document specifies the parties who are involved, what assets are considered under the terms of the trust and how those assets are to be transferred at your death. Everything is spelled out just the way you want it; you call all the shots.

The living trust can be either *revocable* (you can change it any time you like) or *irrevocable* (once set up, it cannot be changed). We are more interested here in the revocable living trust. While it does not have certain tax advantages that the irrevocable trust has, it *does* leave you in total control. The revocable living trust can be changed in any respect or canceled anytime you like. And you always have complete control over your assets.

Parties Involved in the Living Trust

Trustee. Every trust requires a trustee. This can be a bank or an individual. The advantage of naming a bank is its permanence as an institution. It will always be there, and it is rigidly controlled as a fiduciary.

The trustee can also be any individual whom you care to name, including yourself. If you name yourself as trustee, you maintain full control over the trust assets—in this case your mutual fund.

Settler. This is you, the person creating the trust.

Beneficiary. This, of course, is the person (or persons) whom you wish to receive the assets of the trust upon your death.

Successor Trustee. In the event you name yourself as trustee, another person, or a bank, must be named to dispose of the assets under the terms of the trust.

For utmost simplicity and speed, the so-called *one-party trust* can be set up. In this arrangement, you, the creator of the trust (the settler), name yourself as trustee. In a *declaration of trust,* you specifically identify the mutual fund involved and declare that you are holding it in trust for a specified beneficiary. You also designate that beneficiary as the successor trustee, with instructions that upon your death that individual is to turn the mutual fund over to himself or herself, thereby terminating the trust.

While officially there are four jobs, in fact only two people are involved. The settler and trustee are the same person (you), and the successor trustee and beneficiary are the same person (whom you designate). No lawyers, executors, administrators or probate courts are involved. There is no two-to-five-year delay, no 10 percent or more in expenses and no publicity.

How To Set Up a Living Trust

Your attorney will be happy to draw up an individualized trust instrument if you have a unique situation. A custom-tailored document can be expensive, so be sure to ask how much it will cost.

Standard forms with complete instructions are available in the book, *How To Avoid Probate,* by Norman F. Dacey (New York: Crown Publishers, Inc., 1983). This excellent publication, available in bookstores, provides living trust forms for avoiding probate on your mutual funds, as well as other forms to avoid probate on your home, bank accounts, securities and other assets.

SUMMARY

Whether you die with or without a will, the assets in your estate ordinarily will be subject to the delay, cost and possible publicity of probate court. Use of a simple living trust will eliminate the need for probating whatever assets you elect to hold in the trust. The trust can be set up by you at no cost, through the use of standardized forms, or by your attorney. Such assets as mutual funds, bank accounts, securities and real estate can be held in trust to avoid the probate process. If you wish, you can name yourself as trustee and a beneficiary as successor trustee. The trust can be changed or terminated at any time.

CHAPTER 22

Research Information You Can Get Easily

Whether you intend to make just a single mutual fund investment or plan to maintain an ongoing investment program, it is important to have available complete and accurate information. Only then is sound judgment possible.

One way to obtain good information is to contact all the funds listed in our directory and ask them to send you prospectuses and other material (which they will gladly do) and then undertake your own analytical studies. But why reinvent the wheel? There are hundreds of professional analysts who spend all their working hours doing just that. And the results of their efforts are often available to you—and in many instances, at no cost.

Most public libraries subscribe to one or more mutual fund research services. The larger libraries will have several. Each service takes its own approach, but they all strive for accuracy and completeness. And they usually are written in a style that is easy for the nonprofessional, part-time investor to understand. I recommend you look these services over and use the ones that suit you best. A little study will give you the confidence you need to trust in your own judgment. This will generally work out much better than investing on a tip, someone else's enthusiasm or the advice of a salesperson who will earn a commission from your decision.

Perhaps you want the convenience of a personal copy of one or more services. Some services, such as the special editions of *Barron's* and *Forbes,* are inexpensive; others can be quite pricey. Thus, make use of your public library, at least initially.

Following are some of the leading publications and services that have gained the widest appeal.

MAGAZINE PUBLICATIONS

Barron's
This is a national business and financial weekly available by subscription and at newsstands.

Weekly: Publishes annual and weekly price ranges and closing prices, weekly change, latest income and capital gains distributions with record and payment dates and distributions for the last 12 months. Includes Lipper mutual fund performance average for major fund types. Also lists taxable and tax-free money market funds, with asset size, average maturity of securities and seven-day yields.

Quarterly: Publishes special mutual fund sections in February, May, August and November, featuring the Lipper Gauge of Mutual Fund Performance, with individual fund performance, list of averages, quarterly winners and losers and industry news.

Forbes
The Annual Mutual Fund Ratings, published each year in September (available by subscription and at newsstands), features detailed review and performance evaluations of individual funds showing total return, yield, assets, sales charges and annual expenses. It groups funds in categories: stock funds, balanced funds, foreign stock funds, foreign bond funds, bond and preferred stock funds, municipal bond funds and money market funds. A listing of fund distributors is also provided.

RESEARCH AND STATISTICAL SERVICES

CDA/Wiesenberger   CDA Investment Technologies, Inc.
Investment Companies   1355 Piccard Drive
Service   Rockville, MD 20850
                            800-232-2285

This service includes the annual volume *Wiesenberger Investment Companies Service* and the monthly *Mutual Funds Update. Investment Companies* is a 1,200-page, hardcover reference volume published each spring. As the bible of the industry for over 50 years, *Investment Com-*

panies is the most complete single source of information on investment companies. It covers over 4,300 mutual funds, money market funds, unit investment trusts, variable annuity separate accounts and closed-end companies. *Mutual Funds Update* provides a performance review and analysis on mutual funds, money market funds and closed-end funds. It also includes *Panorama,* an annual directory and guide to mutual funds. *Panorama* features ten years of performance information and shareholder data, including fees and expenses, investment minimums, special services, addresses, telephone numbers and investment advisors.

Donoghue's Mutual	IBC/Donoghue
Funds Almanac,	290 Eliot Street
Moneyletter and *Money*	Box 91004
Fund Directory	Ashland, MA 01721-9104
	800-343-5413

Designed for individual and corporate investors, the *Almanac* ($39.95) and *Directory* ($29.95) include performance figures and other information on more than 1,900 no-load, low-load and load funds. No closed-end funds are included. *Moneyletter* ($109 per year) is published twice a month.

Guide to Mutual	Investment Company Institute
Funds/Mutual Fund	1600 M Street, NW
Fact Book	Suite 600
	Washington, DC 20036
	202-293-7700

The Investment Company Institute is the national association of the American mutual fund industry. The guide contains general information on mutual funds and lists more than 2,700 funds that are members of the institute. The *Fact Book* is a basic guide to mutual fund industry trends and statistics.

The Handbook	The No-Load Fund Investor
for No-Load Fund	P. O. Box 283
Investors	Hastings-on-Hudson, NY 10706
	800-252-2042
	914-693-7420

This handbook includes up-to-date performance and investment data on over 1,100 no-load and low-load mutual funds. Published annually, *The Handbook for No-Load Fund Investors* ($45.00) can be supplemented with 12 monthly *No-Load Fund Investor* newsletters.

Johnson's Charts   Johnson's Charts, Inc.
                              175 Bridle Path
                              Williamsville, NY 14221
                              716-626-0845

This service publishes graphs and charts analyzing long-term performance of individual mutual funds. Included is information on historical income and capital gains payments, share price trends and total returns with and without dividend reinvestments.

Lipper Analytical   Lipper Analytical Services, Inc.
Services, Inc.   47 Maple Street, Suite 101
                              Summit, NJ 07901
                              908-273-2772

Lipper provides statistical services on the mutual fund industry. It is widely quoted and used by other financial publications.

The Mutual Fund   Perritt Investments, Inc.
Encyclopedia   680 N. Lake Shore Drive
                              Tower Suite 2038
                              Chicago, IL 60611

This annual publication profiles nearly 1,300 no-load, low-load and load funds. Each profile gives a detailed statement of objectives and strategies and provides key financial statistics, including assets under management, current yield, portfolio turnover ratio, risk factors and year-by-year and five-year total returns. To avoid decision making further, the minimum initial investment for each fund is noted as well as the cost of investing in each fund and the company address and toll-free number.

Mutual Fund Profiles   Standard & Poor's Corporation
                              25 Broadway
                              New York, NY 10004
                              800-221-5277
                              212-208-8805

This publication is produced jointly with Lipper Analytical Services, Inc. Individual mutual fund profiles include statistical data; investment policy, performance and evaluation; comparison with S&P 500 results; and top holdings.

United Mutual   Babson-United Investment
Fund Selector   Advisors, Inc.
                         101 Prescott Street
                         Wellesley Hills, MA 02181-3319
                         617-235-0900

In addition to mutual fund industry news and views, this publication lists current yields and performance results on a wide range of funds. Data is broken down into major fund groups, top performers in each fund category and by load, no-load and low-load funds. The *United Mutual Fund Selector* is published semimonthly ($125 per year).

SUMMARY

It has been said that anyone can become an expert in almost anything in six months. That may be stretching it a bit, but it is true that most investors will find it surprisingly easy to become competent in mutual funds by utilizing the information in this book, visiting a local public library for research information and calling mutual fund companies for prospectuses and other material they gladly make available. Don't be afraid to step out. You can do it!

CHAPTER 23

How To Calculate Taxable Gains and Losses

Whenever you sell or exchange mutual fund shares, you may have a capital gain or loss that must be reported to the Internal Revenue Service (IRS) at tax time. A capital gain or loss may be realized when you:

- sell shares of a fund,
- write a check on a fund or
- exchange from one fund into another.

To calculate your gains and losses, it is necessary to know your cost basis. *Cost basis* is the term used by the IRS for the amount of money you have invested in your mutual fund shares. If you sell for more than your cost basis, you have a gain; if you sell for less than your cost basis, you have a loss.

You can use four different methods to calculate your mutual fund cost basis, and from that your gains and losses. It is relatively easy to calculate your gains and losses once you have determined your cost basis and selling price. Incidentally, capital gains and losses generally do not apply to money market funds—as long as your money market fund has no sales load and maintains a constant $1 per-share price.

TAX AND ACCOUNT RECORDS YOU WILL NEED

To report gains and losses on your tax return, you must know which shares you sold, how long you held them and their purchase and sale prices. For this purpose, keep records of the following:

- The date of each purchase, sale or exchange of shares
- The number of shares purchased or sold in each transaction
- The price per share at which shares were bought or sold
- The total dollar amount involved in each transaction
- Any sales charges, commissions or redemption fees paid

If dividend or capital gains distributions are reinvested in your account, each reinvestment is counted as a purchase or as shares. Be sure to keep records of all reinvestments, as they will be needed at tax time. Save all your account statements and confirmation statements. Most mutual funds send year-end summary statements, and *all* must send Form 1099-B by January 31 of each year. The funds can also provide you with historical data on your account if you lose your records; however, there may be a charge for this service.

METHODS FOR CALCULATING COST BASIS

Calculating your cost basis begins with determining the purchase price for all shares you own in a particular fund. You may have made many different purchases at various share prices. Reinvested dividend and capital gains distributions, as well as additions to your account, are all separate transactions.

When you sell your shares and want to figure what your gains and losses are, you need a way to determine the cost of the different shares you own. And, if you sell only a part of your shares, you need a way of determining which shares you sold. The IRS permits the following four accounting methods for determining the cost basis for mutual fund shares:

1. The *first-in, first-out (FIFO)* method is probably the most popular, and it is the standard used by the IRS. Under FIFO, you simply assume that the first shares you sell are the first shares you bought.
2. The *specific shares* method lets you identify exactly which shares you are selling. This gives you maximum flexibility, but you must identify the shares in advance of their sale. If you have already sold them, it is too late to use the specific shares method for that transaction.
3. The *average cost–single category* method averages the cost of all your shares regardless of the holding period.

4. The *average cost–double category* method allows you to calculate two average cost figures: (1) short-term shares owned one year or less and (2) long-term shares owned for more than one year.

Beginning in 1991, the highest marginal federal income tax rate became 31 percent; however, long-term capital gains are subject to a maximum 28 percent tax rate. If you are in a high tax bracket, you can save on taxes by trying to maximize long-term capital gains.

Average cost methods 2 and 3 have certain special requirements. First, you must state which method you have chosen in your tax return; once chosen, you must use that same method for all your accounts in the same name in that mutual fund. (You can't change to another method without IRS permission.) Second, the average cost methods are available only for mutual funds; they can't be used for other investments, such as individual stocks or bonds.

An average cost method may make sense if you have made a number of purchases over a long period of time. If you trade frequently, however, your average cost per share can change every time you buy more shares at a new price. It is important to keep your records up-to-date.

REINVESTED DIVIDENDS OR CAPITAL GAINS

Remember that each time you reinvest dividends or capital gains distributions, you are actually buying additional shares that add to the cost basis of your account. This is also true of so-called directed dividend programs, under which dividends are automatically sent from one mutual fund into shares of another.

Your cost basis for shares purchased by reinvestment equals the total amount of the dividend or capital gain you received. You must take this additional amount into account when calculating your cost basis.

LOAD FUNDS

If you buy a mutual fund that has a sales charge (load), include the sales charge paid as part of your cost basis. For example, if you sent $1,000 to a fund with a 6 percent sales charge, you would pay a sales load of $60. Your cost basis would be the full $1,000 you sent to the fund, not the net amount of $940.

The price per share quoted by a mutual fund usually includes the sales charge, so you don't have to make a separate calculation. If you buy a no-load mutual fund from a broker, however, you may pay a separate sales charge or commission on top of the share price you are quoted. Include this amount in your purchase price to calculate your cost basis correctly.

DEFERRED SALES CHARGES AND REDEMPTION FEES

Certain mutual funds impose *deferred* sales charges and redemption fees. Such charges should be taken into account when you sell mutual fund shares, for determining gains and losses.

You can calculate these charges in either of two ways: (1) by subtracting them from your sales proceeds or (2) by adding them to your cost basis. The method you use will depend on how your mutual fund reports the sales proceeds on Form 1099-B, which reports your sales for the year. The sales proceeds you report on your tax return should correspond with the proceeds reported on Form 1099-B so that the IRS can compare your tax return and the Form 1099-B information they have on file.

If your mutual fund group reports net sales proceeds, then your deferred sales charges have already been subtracted from your proceeds, and you can report the net amount on your tax return. If, on the other hand, your mutual fund group reports gross proceeds or both amounts, report the gross amount on your tax return and add the charges to your cost basis instead. In either case, your gain or loss is the same. But by making sure your tax return and your Form 1099-B totals agree, you avoid having to explain any discrepancy on your tax return.

WASH SALES

If you sell shares at a loss and buy additional shares in the same mutual fund within 30 days after (or before) the sale, you can't take the loss on your tax return until you sell the additional shares. The IRS considers the additional shares as having "washed" your loss.

Although you can't take the loss on your original shares, the IRS does allow you to add the loss to your cost basis for the additional shares. When you eventually do sell the additional shares, your gain or loss will reflect the loss on the original shares.

LONG-TERM CAPITAL GAINS DISTRIBUTIONS

If your fund distributes a long-term capital gains distribution on your shares and you sell those shares at a loss after holding them for six months or less, you may have to treat some or all of your loss as a long-term capital loss. For each share you have sold, the amount that must be treated as long-term loss equals the amount of long-term capital gains distributions you received on that share. Long-term capital gains distributions are reported to you annually in box 1C of Form 1099-DIV.

See Chapter 19, "Timing Your Purchases To Avoid Taxes," for information on how to reduce exposure to income taxes.

MERGED FUNDS

In recent years, many mutual funds have been merged. If you have owned one of the funds that was merged into another fund, your holding period and total cost basis are not affected by the merger. Since the new fund most likely has a different price per share, however, you will have a new share balance. When figuring gains and losses, you must do some recalculations to reflect the correct number of shares in each transaction.

Your cost basis per share in the new fund is your old total cost basis divided by your new number of shares. Use this new cost basis per share and new share balance in figuring any gains or losses for transactions after the merger took place.

GIFTS OR INHERITANCES

If you have received shares as a gift, your cost basis depends on the value of the shares on the date of the gift and the donor's cost basis, as well as your sales price. The cost basis of inherited shares is generally the value of the shares on the date that the decedent died.

FOR ADDITIONAL INFORMATION

The IRS publishes a number of booklets to assist taxpayers in completing tax returns. You can order IRS Publication 550 (*Investment Income and Expense*), Publication 551 (*Basis of Assets*) and Publication 564 (*Mutual Fund Distributions*). They are available at no charge from the IRS by calling 1-800-TAX-FORM.

SUMMARY

It is relatively easy to calculate your taxable gains and losses, but it is important to maintain a file of all your account statements. You will need to know which shares you sold, how long you held them and their purchase and sale prices. You may use any of the four accounting methods permitted by the IRS, but be sure that the one you select is used consistently.

PART FOUR

Tax-Advantaged Retirement Plans for Your Business

CHAPTER 24

Advantages of a Qualified Retirement Plan

Tax-qualified retirement plans (pension and profit-sharing plans) may be adopted by sole proprietors, partnerships and corporations. A qualified retirement program includes both the investments and services necessary to establish and maintain qualified retirement plans.

TAX ADVANTAGES

You and your employees may benefit in three important ways from the tax advantages in a qualified retirement plan:

1. **Tax-deductible contributions.** Employer contributions to the plan are deductible for federal income tax purposes and are not currently includable in employees' taxable income.
2. **Tax-deferred earnings.** All earnings on plan contributions accumulate on a tax-deferred basis. This means that earnings grow free from federal income taxation until distribution.
3. **Tax-favored distributions.** Lump-sum distributions from the plans may be eligible for special tax treatment called *forward averaging*. In most cases this will result in significant tax savings.

TAX-DEFERRED COMPOUNDING OF EARNINGS

Assume that $20,000 is contributed each year to your account (the maximum allowable contribution is $30,000) for 25 years in a qualified pension or profit-sharing plan. If your account earns 9 percent each year, under the tax-deferred plan its final value will be $1,846,480. (See Figure 24.1.)

If, on the other hand, you don't take advantage of a qualified plan, here's what will happen. Assuming that you are in the 31 percent tax bracket and invest $20,000 each year of taxable earnings, you are in effect limited to investing only $13,800 of after-tax dollars for your retirement savings. And, your investment earnings on these savings will be further reduced each year by income taxes. As a result, in 25 years your account will be worth only $1,200,488.

Of course, the amounts in your qualified plan's account will be taxed when you withdraw them. Nevertheless, even after you pay taxes on your distributions, there are two reasons you should enjoy a substantially higher retirement income than you would through a conventional, taxable savings plan. First, you may be in a lower tax bracket during your retirement years. And second, you will be starting your retirement with a larger accumulated sum. Assuming your tax-deferred account continues to earn 9 percent and you are then still in the 31 percent tax bracket, you will receive $40,116 (after taxes) more per year in earnings than you would from the nonqualified retirement account.

Mutual funds offer a broad range of services and investments that make it easy to establish and administer a tax-qualified retirement plan. They are as follows:

FIGURE 24.1

	Tax-Qualified Plan	Nonqualified Plan
Net annual contribution	$ 20,000	$ 13,800
Total contributions in 25 years	500,000	345,000
Net earnings in 25 years (at 9 percent)	1,346,480	855,488
Value of account in 25 years	1,846,480	1,200,488
Annual after-tax earnings at retirement (at 9 percent)	114,666	74,550

- **Prototype plans and trust documents.** These documents have been determined by the Internal Revenue Service (IRS) to satisfy the requirements in the tax laws for qualified retirement plans, including the many special requirements arising from the Tax Reform Act of 1986.
- **Multiple adoption agreements.** Simplified adoption agreements make it easy to adopt a pension plan, a money purchase pension plan or both.
- **Numerous investment options.** You may select from a broad range of investments, from aggressive common stock mutual funds to conservative, income-oriented bond and money market funds.
- **Complete participant direction.** Under many plans, participating employees are permitted to self-direct the investment of their individual plan accounts. Exchange privileges permit participants to change their mutual fund selections as their objectives and perception of the marketplace change.
- **Record keeping/participant accounting.** The mutual fund will automatically credit contributions to employees' individual plan accounts and maintain up-to-date records of each account's status, reflecting all contributions, earnings and distributions.
- **Trustee Services.** As an employer, you have the option of appointing a trust company or individual (including yourself) as trustee.
- **Tax reporting.** Some funds will arrange for you to be provided with consolidated financial information to complete your plan's annual report to the IRS (Form 5500). They can also make distribution or withdrawal payments to employees upon your instructions and issue the necessary IRS tax forms. These tax-reporting services are normally available only if the plan trustee is connected with the fund.

MUTUAL FUNDS AS INVESTMENTS

The popularity of using mutual fund shares in employee benefit plans has accelerated as the use of common stocks in retirement plans has become more widespread. There is a desire to provide protection against the effects of inflation on long-term investment programs. Many companies, large and small, also feel that it is desirable for their employees to have a stake in business profits. The employee who wishes to direct part of his or her retirement funds into common stocks or fixed-income securities can have broad diversification and continuous investment management.

Employers are able to serve as trustees of their pension and/or profit-sharing plan(s), whether they have any special investment knowledge or not. Therefore, they can keep control of the plans and still avoid the responsibility for investment decisions.

Through mutual funds, trustees of retirement plans can obtain the particular type of investment policy they want, with full knowledge of how the policy has worked out in the past. And they can be certain that the same policy can be followed throughout the life of the plan, both when the investment size may be small in the beginning and later as the plan grows to substantial size.

SUMMARY

Additional advantages of mutual funds include the ease with which shares can be evaluated and the simplicity of distributing a withdrawing participant's share of the retirement plan assets. If the plan provides for it, a retiring or departing employee may receive mutual fund shares rather than cash. Such an arrangement provides a convenient means of making the distribution. Under this approach, the individual is not faced with making an investment decision upon receiving a substantial amount of cash. If the retiree or other beneficiary is to be paid in cash, mutual fund shares can be sold with little or no disruption to the underlying portfolio.

The deductibility of contributions and tax-sheltered accumulation of earnings are two basic reasons why profitable business concerns choose to maintain qualified retirement plans. However, such plans also tend to provide an incentive for employees to stay with a company. When plan participants terminate employment, any nonvested benefits they leave behind will often be divided among the remaining participants or used to reduce future employer contributions. Mutual funds provide a convenient and cost-effective way to have the invested funds professionally managed.

CHAPTER 25

Qualified Pension and Profit-Sharing Plans

Many mutual fund companies now offer complete, flexible and carefully designed tax-qualified retirement programs. They provide for multiple plan selection and offer an exceptionally diverse range of investment options.

You may obtain, without charge, qualified retirement plans that meet all current standards under federal tax law. If you already have a plan and it has not been amended to reflect the changes arising from the Tax Reform Act of 1986 or if it has been discontinued, you can easily bring the plan into compliance by transferring it to a mutual fund company.

You can expect high-quality service from your mutual fund at little or no cost. A phone call will bring you a complete kit for setting up a qualified retirement plan. (Use the fund's 800 number.) It will typically include the following:

- A qualified retirement plan booklet containing plan highlights, answers to frequently asked questions, plan documents and IRS opinion letters
- Booklets that contain the adoption agreements and other material you will need to adopt the plan
- Information on the specific mutual fund(s) you are interested in and a brochure describing all the currently available funds in the company's family of funds

QUALIFIED RETIREMENT PLANS

You may generally select from three different plans to meet your particular needs:

1. **Profit-sharing plan.** Contributions may be made whether or not your business shows a profit, and the percentage you contribute is discretionary. The deduction for participants' contributions generally is limited to 15 percent of employed compensation (or 13.04 percent of self-employed income).
2. **Money purchase pension plan.** Contributions are required annually and must be equal to a fixed percentage of each participant's compensation, regardless of profits. The maximum deduction is effectively the lesser of 25 percent of the participant's compensation or $30,000 (or 20 percent of net earnings for self-employed persons).
3. **Combination of the profit-sharing and money purchase pension plans.** This is the most flexible arrangement. You may provide for combined contributions of up to the maximum deductible amount (i.e., the lesser of 25 percent of compensation or $30,000) while retaining the flexibility through the profit-sharing plan to contribute lesser amounts. (Deductible contributions for self-employed individuals are limited to 20 percent of net earnings.)

When setting up a qualified retirement plan, you may appoint a trust company as trustee or any other corporate or individual trustee (such as yourself). The simplified adoption agreements provided by the mutual fund will fulfill most employer's needs. However, alternative adoption agreements that include additional plan options, such as more restrictive coverage provisions, vesting schedules and Social Security integration, are also available.

THE PROTOTYPE RETIREMENT PLAN

When adopting a *prototype retirement plan* provided by a mutual fund, you can expect that complex technical and legal aspects of the plan will be precise and up-to-date and will be amended as necessary following any tax law changes. The features and benefits you should receive from your mutual fund retirement plan include the following:

- **Investment choice for self-direction.** Plan participants may direct their investments among a variety of funds in the mutual fund family. Whether your investment goals are aggressive, moderate or conservative (or somewhere in between), you can pursue your objectives.
- **High-quality account service.** Long-term investing, inherent in retirement planning, requires long-term and high-quality service. Mutual funds will issue easy-to-read account statements on a regular basis to keep you current on your plan's progress. At year-end, your fund should be able to provide consolidated financial information for use in completing the plan's annual report to the IRS (Form 5500).
- **Low cost.** Top mutual fund companies operate at very efficient expense ratios (annual expenses as a percentage of net assets), which means that a high proportion of your investment's gross income is carried down to the bottom line. For example, the expense ratio for all Vanguard funds was 0.35 in 1990, less than a third of the average of other major mutual fund complexes, according to Lipper Analytical Services, Inc.
- **Toll-free assistance and personal service.** Many mutual funds permit you and your plan participants to call toll-free on any business day for answers to questions about your plan and their funds. Or the plan administrator may call for assistance with changes or problems that may arise.

DESIGNING YOUR RETIREMENT PLAN

Employee Eligibility.   In determining who shall be eligible to participate in your qualified retirement plan, you may require all employees to have attained a minimum age (up to age 21) and/or have completed a minimum period of service (up to two years). You are also permitted to limit coverage under your plan to certain groups or categories of employees, provided that the Internal Revenue Code's nondiscrimination requirements are satisfied. Of course, you may elect not to impose any eligibility requirements, in which case all employees will be immediately eligible.

Employee Vesting.   Participating employees will become vested in their plan accounts according to the vesting schedule you select. As an alternative to full (100 percent) and immediate vesting, you may provide any vesting schedule (i.e., 5-year cliff vesting, 7-year graded vesting) that meets the statutory requirements of the Internal Revenue Code.

Integration with Social Security.   You may provide a formula for integrating the allocation of employer contributions with Social Security. This will allow you to combine the employer's Social Security contributions with its plan contributions to permit greater contributions (as a percentage of total compensation) to the plan for higher-paid employees.

Plan Investments.   You may permit plan participants to self-direct the investment of their separate accounts under the plan, or you may provide that the plan administrator shall be responsible for directing the investment of all plan accounts. Investments may include a mix of stock, bond, balanced and money market funds.

SETTING UP YOUR PLAN

To participate in a qualified retirement program, you should follow six basic steps:

1.   **Consult with your attorney or tax adviser.** Before adopting a prototype-defined contribution plan as your money purchase pension plan or profit-sharing plan (or both), first meet with your attorney or tax adviser to determine whether the specific plan or combination of plans you have selected is appropriate in view of your particular circumstances.
2.   **Complete the adoption agreement.** Complete the appropriate money purchase pension plan or profit-sharing plan adoption agreement. Detailed instructions will be provided for you with the forms. If you have any questions, call the fund. At most funds, a representative of the mutual fund will be glad to assist you.
3.   **Adopt the plan documents.** As employer, you should formally adopt the appropriate prototype plan, trust agreement and adoption agreement *no later than the end of the first plan year.* For corporations, the forms booklet provided by the fund will usually

provide sample boards of directors resolutions authorizing the adoption of these documents.

4. **Notify employees and distribute participant election forms.** Announce to all your employees the establishment of your plan with its important provisions. Distribute election forms that may be used to designate beneficiaries and direct investments. The forms booklet will normally include a sample participant election form.

5. **Complete the contribution investment form.** Using the information supplied by your employees on their election forms, complete the contribution investment form and send it to your mutual fund along with the completed adoption agreement and a check for your initial plan contribution.

6. **Provide notice to interested parties and a summary plan description** to all plan participants who are common-law employees. (Plans of partnerships that cover only partners and their spouses as well as plans of sole proprietors that cover only the sole proprietor and his or her spouse are exempt from this requirement.) **Obtain a fidelity bond.**

SUMMARY

Qualified profit-sharing, money purchase pension and combination profit-sharing/money purchase pension plans are available from many mutual fund companies. They provide prototype plans that have been preapproved as to form by the IRS. The fund administrators are usually happy to assist in completing the necessary forms and getting your plan in operation. It is always wise to consult with your attorney or tax adviser before implementing a qualified retirement plan.

The Simplified Employee Pension (SEP) Plan

If you are self-employed, own a small company or business or have a professional practice, a *simplified employee pension (SEP)* plan provides a retirement plan that offers *considerable tax benefits* and is *easy to administer.*

KEY FEATURES OF A SEP

SEP plans have the following five features:

1. You can *deduct,* from current federally taxable income, contributions of up to $30,000 per person (to a limit of 15 percent of employed compensation or 13.04 percent of self-employed income). And you can make your regular IRA contribution in addition, for a total contribution of $32,000! (Note that depending on your tax bracket, your IRA contribution may not be fully deductible.)
2. Contributions are simply made to your individual retirement account (IRA) and to the IRA of each covered employee.
3. Annual contributions are discretionary, so you can skip some years if you wish.

4. All earnings on SEP contributions accumulate in your IRA (or in your employees' IRAs) on a tax-deferred basis. Earnings grow free of taxation until actual distribution.
5. Compared to a qualified retirement plan, a SEP plan is virtually free of paperwork.

For example, if you are self-employed, in the 31 percent tax bracket and contribute $20,000 per year under a SEP for the next 25 years, here is how your investment can grow:

	Invested in a SEP-IRA	Invested with No Tax Shelter
Total amount contributed	$ 500,000	$ 500,000
Tax savings (in 31 percent bracket)	–155,000	0
Net after-tax contribution	$ 345,000	$ 500,000
Value of your IRA account after 25 years (assuming 9 percent return per year)	$1,846,480	$1,200,488

Taxes must be paid on withdrawals taken from an IRA. But even if you took the entire balance as a lump-sum distribution taxed at 31 percent, your net after-tax return is still more than $73,000 higher than the no-tax-shelter plan. In addition, you will have saved $155,000 through the tax deductibility of your contributions.

The beauty of a SEP is that you get these benefits under a plan that is about as simple as a regular IRA.

ADMINISTRATION OF A SEP

Just two steps are needed to administer a SEP:

1. Furnish each covered employee with a copy of a completed SEP-IRA contribution agreement.
2. Give every employee a statement each year showing the SEP amount contributed to his or her IRA.

There is no IRS Form 5500, no Department of Labor filings and no complicated plan and trust documents.

ADDITIONAL BENEFITS OF A SEP

Investment flexibility.   The SEP allows you (and your SEP partici-pants) to self-direct your investment among the large number of different mutual funds appropriate for retirement investing.

Low cost.   There are no sales charges for investing in any no-load mutual fund. Annual custodial fees charged by such mutual funds usually range from $10 to $25.

LIMITATIONS OF A SEP

A SEP has certain limitations that may make other types of retire-ment plans more appropriate, particularly for larger corporations.

Lack of employer control over employee retirement savings. Employer contributions under a SEP are deposited directly in the IRAs established for covered employees. These contributions are vested im-mediately and may be withdrawn by employees at any time (subject to the IRA rules that generally impose a 10 percent penalty on distributions prior to age $59\frac{1}{2}$). The lack of employer control may limit the SEP as a vehicle for binding employees to the sponsoring employer.

Strict coverage requirements.   A SEP must cover all employees over age 21 who have performed any service for an employer during any three of the past five years (except for certain union employees and employees who have earned less than $300, as indexed, in a year). This means that contributions under a SEP may be required on behalf of part-time and temporary employees even if they work less than 1,000 hours a year. It is possible to impose stricter coverage and eligibility requirements under a qualified pension or profit-sharing plan.

No favorable tax treatment for lump-sum distributions.   All SEP funds that are distributed from an employee's IRA will be taxed as ordinary income. Thus, SEP monies are not eligible for the special five-year forward-averaging taxation that applies to certain lump-sum distributions from qualified pension and profit-sharing plans. Of course, this limitation does not affect people who elect to receive their retirement plan distributions in installments over their retirement rather than in a lump sum.

No loans permitted.   Employees are not permitted to borrow from the SEP monies that are deposited in their IRAs. In contrast, employees may be permitted to borrow from certain types of qualified pension and profit-sharing plans, although loans from Keogh plans to sole proprietors or partners and loans from plans of Subchapter S corporations to shareholder-employees are generally not permitted. Thus, only regular corporation employers possibly forego the opportunity for retirement plan loans by adopting a SEP instead of a qualified pension or profit-sharing plan.

Fifteen percent of compensation limit.   Under a SEP, the maximum contribution on behalf of any individual is the lesser of $30,000 or 15 percent of compensation (or 13.04 percent of self-employment income). In contrast, under a money purchase plan, the maximum contribution amount is the lesser of $30,000 or 25 percent of compensation (or 20 percent of self-employment income). Thus, for certain individuals, greater contributions may be made under a money purchase plan than under a SEP. However, one price you pay with a money purchase pension plan is the loss of flexibility. Under that type of plan, employer contributions are not discretionary and must be made each year regardless of profits or earnings.

SUMMARY

The SEP provides a retirement plan with considerable tax benefits, and it is easy to administer. It is generally appropriate for a person who is self-employed, has a small company or business or maintains a professional practice.

CHAPTER 27

Which Is the Best Retirement Plan for Your Business?

There are important differences between the various types of retirement plans established by law. This chapter considers some of the key bottom-line issues you may want to consider. A careful review of the four different approaches, for which mutual fund companies have prototype retirement plans, will help you to decide which plan is best for you. I strongly recommend that you confer with your attorney or tax adviser before making a decision.

Many no-load mutual fund companies offer all the plans discussed below, and they generally will provide you with assistance in setting up your tax-sheltered retirement program and commission-free investing of your plan assets.

COMPARING QUALIFIED RETIREMENT PLANS AND THE SEP-IRA

Maximum Tax-Deductible Contribution Per Employee

- **Money purchase pension plan.** The lesser of $30,000 or 25 percent of employed compensation (20 percent of self-employed income*).

---

* When determining self-employed income, net earnings should be reduced by the amount of deductible self-employment taxes.

- **Profit-sharing plan.** The lesser of $30,000 or 15 percent of employed compensation (13.04 percent of self-employed income*).
- **Combined money purchase pension and profit-sharing plans.** The lesser of $30,000 or 25 percent of employed compensation (20 percent of self-employed income*).
- **Simplified employee pension (SEP)–IRA.** The lesser of $30,000 or 15 percent of employed compensation (13.04 percent of self-employed income).

Relative Advantages

- **Money purchase pension plan.** Provides the highest possible contribution. It is a qualified plan and allows for tax-favored forward averaging on lump-sum distributions and loans to employees (but generally not to owners). A vesting schedule is permitted.
- **Profit-sharing plan.** Annual contributions are discretionary; you can skip some years if you wish. It is a qualified plan and allows for forward averaging and loans to employees (but generally not to owners). A vesting schedule is permitted.
- **Combined money purchase and profit-sharing plans.** Provides flexibility and maximum contribution. You can contribute up to 15 percent of compensation to the profit-sharing plan (discretionary) and up to 10 percent to the money purchase plan (mandatory) for a total of up to 25 percent. These are qualified plans and allow for forward averaging and loans to employees (but generally not to owners). Vesting schedules are permitted.
- **SEP-IRA.** There is virtually no paperwork. Provides full tax benefits for deductible contributions and tax-deferred growth of assets with a plan that's easy to understand and administer. Annual contributions are discretionary; you can skip any year if you wish. Your plan may be adopted for a tax year up to the tax return filing deadline (usually April 15).

---

* When determining self-employed income, net earnings should be reduced by the amount of deductible self-employment taxes.

Relative Disadvantages

- **Money purchase pension plan.** The plan must be adopted by the end of the tax year (usually December 31). There is no flexibility on contributions; you must contribute the stated percentage each year, subject to penalties. Administrative and filing requirements can be quite extensive and often require professional assistance. These requirements include the IRS Form 5500, a multi-page report that must be filed annually. There are also Department of Labor reporting and disclosure requirements if you have employees.
- **Profit-sharing plan.** The plan must be adopted by the end of the tax year (usually December 31). Administrative and filing requirements can be quite extensive and often require professional assistance. The requirements include the IRS Form 5500, a multi-page report that must be filed annually. There are also Department of Labor reporting and disclosure requirements if you have employees.
- **Combined money purchase pension and profit-sharing plans.** The plans must be adopted by the end of the tax year (usually December 31). You have adopted *two* plans, each of which requires all the forms and reports mentioned above in connection with money purchase pension and profit-sharing plans.
- **SEP-IRA.** There are no forward-averaging tax advantages for lump-sum distributions. However, in many cases the usefulness of this benefit is quite limited. No vesting schedule is permitted in SEP-IRAs.

SUMMARY

Each of the four basic retirement plans has certain advantages and disadvantages. They should be carefully evaluated and discussed with your attorney or tax adviser. The mutual fund company you select can be very helpful in guiding you to a successful implementation and administration of your plan.

APPENDIXES

APPENDIX A

No-Load Mutual Funds—By Investment Objective

The funds in this listing are grouped by primary investment objective. A directory of all the funds, with addresses and both in-state and out-of-state telephone numbers, follows this listing. Their representatives will be happy to mail you a prospectus for each fund in which you may have an interest. Every effort has been made to include only funds that carry no sales charges, redemption fees or significant annual 12b-1 charges. However, to be sure, always read the prospectus carefully before investing.

Maximum Capital Gains

Advantage Special Fund
Afuture Fund
Boston Company Special
  Growth Fund
Columbia Special Fund
Crabbe Hudson Growth Fund
Dreyfus New Leaders Fund
Evergreen Fund
Fiduciary Management
  Associates
Financial Dynamics Fund
First Eagle Fund of America
Flex Growth Fund
Founders Frontier Fund
Founders Special Fund

Gintel Capital Appreciation
  Fund
Lexington Worldwide Emerging
  Markets
Maxus Equity Fund
Merriman Timed Capital
  Appreciation
Neuwirth Fund
Perritt Capital Growth Fund
Prudent Speculator Leveraged
  Fund
Rainbow Fund
Rushmore Nova
Scudder Development Fund
Selected Special Shares
Sequoia Fund
Shadow Stock Fund

Sherman Dean
Stein Roe Capital Opportunities
  Fund
Tocqueville Fund
Twentieth Century Growth
  Investors
Twentieth Century Ultra
  Investors
USAA Aggressive Growth Fund
Value Line Leveraged Growth
  Investors
Value Line Special Situations
  Fund
WPG Tudor Fund

Small-Company Growth

Acorn Fund
Alger Small Capitalization
  Portfolio
Counsellors Emerging Growth
Eclipse Equity Fund
Fasciano Fund
GIT Equity Trust Special
  Growth Portfolio
Janus Venture Fund
Kaufmann Fund
Legg Mason Special Investment
  Trust
Nicholas Limited Edition
Olympic Trust - Small Capital
Rushmore Over-The-Counter
  Index Plus Fund
Sit New Beginning Growth
  Fund
Southeastern Asset - Small Cap
Sun America Emerging Growth
  Fund
T. Rowe Price New Horizons
  Fund
T. Rowe Price Small-Cap Value
  Fund

Twentieth Century Giftrust
  Investors
Twentieth Century Vista
  Investors
Vanguard Explorer Fund
Vanguard Small Capitalization
  Stock Fund
Wasatch Aggressive Equity
Wasatch Growth Fund
WPG Growth Fund
Wright Junior Blue Chip

Long-Term Growth

AARP Capital Growth Fund
Advantage Growth Fund
Alger Growth Portfolio
Allegro Growth Fund
Armstong Associates
Babson Enterprise Fund
Babson Growth Fund
Baron Asset Fund
Bartlett Capital Fixed Income
  Fund
Bascom Hill Investors
Beacon Hill Mutual Fund
Berwyn Fund
Boston Company Capital
  Appreciation Fund
Boston Company Contrarian
  Fund
Brandywine Fund
CGM Capital Development
  Fund
Clipper Fund
Columbia Growth Fund
Concorde Value Fund
Copley Fund
Counsellors Capital
  Appreciation
Crabbe Huson Equity Fund
Dreman Contrarian Portfolio

Dreyfus Fund
Dreyfus Growth Opportunity
    Fund
Dreyfus Index Fund
Dreyfus Life & Annuity Index
Dreyfus Third Century Fund
Fairmont Fund
Federated Growth Trust
Federated Stock Trust
Fidelity Destiny Plan I
Fidelity Destiny Plan II
Fidelity Disciplined Equity
    Fund
Fidelity Retirement Growth
    Fund
Fidelity Trend Fund
Fidelity U.S. Equity Index
Fidelity Value Fund
Flex Muirfield Fund
Fontaine Capital Appreciation
Founders Discovery Fund
Founders Growth Fund
Gabelli Asset Fund
Gabelli Growth Fund
Galaxy Equity Value Fund
Gateway Growth Plus Fund
General Aggressive Growth
Gintel Fund
Greenspring Fund
Harbor Growth Fund
Helmsman Disciplined Equity
Helmsman Growth Equity
Ivy Growth Fund
Janus Fund
Janus Twenty Fund
Legg Mason Value Trust
Lexington Technical Strategy
    Fund
Mairs & Power Growth Fund
Mathers Fund
Meridian Fund
Mutual Beacon Fund

Neuberger & Berman
    Manhattan Fund
Newton Growth Fund
Nicholas Fund
Northeast Investors Growth
    Fund
Pimit Growth Stock Portfolio
Portico Funds - Special Growth
Prime Value Growth Stock
Regis-DSI Discipline Value
Reich & Tang Equity Fund
SAFECO Growth Fund
SBSF Growth Fund
Schafer Value Fund
Scudder Capital Growth Fund
SEI Institutional Managed-Cap
    Appreciation
Sentry Fund
Sound Shore Fund
Southeastern Asset Value
Special Portfolio - Stock
State Farm Growth Fund
Stein Roe Special Fund
Stein Roe Stock Fund
Stralem Fund
T. Rowe Price Capital
    Appreciation Fund
T. Rowe Price Growth Stock
    Fund
T. Rowe Price New America
    Growth Fund
Twentieth Century Heritage
    Investors
Twentieth Century Select
    Investors
UMB Heartland Fund
UMB Stock Fund
United Service Funds All
    American Equity Fund
United Service Funds Growth
USAA Growth Fund
Valley Forge Fund

Value Line Fund
Vanguard Morgan Growth Fund
Vanguard Primecap Fund
Vanguard Windsor Fund
Vanguard Windsor II
Vanguard World U.S. Growth
    Fund
Variable Stock Fund
Vista Capital Growth
Vista Growth & Income
Volumetric Fund
Wall Street Fund
Wayne Hummer Growth Fund
Weitz Series - Value
William Blair Growth Shares
Wright Selected Blue Chip
    Equities

Growth and Current Income

AARP Growth & Income Fund
American Pension Inv - Total
    Return
BB&K Diversa Fund
Bell Atlantic Mutual - Equity
Blanchard Strategic Growth
Boston Company Asset
    Allocation
Caldwell Fund
Crabbe Huson Asset Allocation
Dodge & Cox Stock Fund
Dreman High Return Portfolio
Dreyfus Convertible Securities
    Fund
Elfun Diversified Fund
Elfun Trusts
Evergreen Total Return Fund
Evergreen Value Timing Fund
Fam Value Fund
FBP Contrarian Fund
Fidelity Asset Manager
Fidelity Fund

Financial Industrial Fund
Financial Industrial Income
    Fund
Founders Blue Chip Fund
Fremont Multi Asset Fund
Gateway Index Plus
GE S & S Program Mutual Fund
Gintel Erisa Fund
Harbor Capital Appreciation
    Fund
Harbor Value Fund
Helmsman Income Equity
IAI Stock Fund
Ivy Growth with Income Fund
Jamestown Fund
Legg Mason Total Return Trust
Lepercq-Istel Fund
Lexington Growth & Income
    Fund
LMH Fund
Merriman Asset Allocation Fund
Merriman Blue Chip Fund
Monetta Fund
Muhlenkamp Fund
National Industries Fund
Neuberger & Berman Guardian
    Fund
Nicholas II
Pine Street Fund
Portico Funds—Equity Index
Portico Funds—Income &
    Growth
Primary Trend Fund
Rushmore Stock Market Index
    Plus Fund
SAFECO Equity Fund
Scudder Growth & Income Fund
SEI Index Funds—S&P 500
SEI Institutional
    Managed—Value
Selected American Shares
Stein Roe Prime Equities

Stein Roe Total Return Fund
Stratton Growth Fund
T. Rowe Price Growth Income
  Fund
Thompson, Unger & Plumb
  Fund
Trustee's Commingled U.S.
  Equity
U.S. Boston Invest—Growth &
  Income
Vanguard Asset Allocation Fund
Vanguard Index Trust Extended
Vanguard Quantitative
  Portfolios
Vanguard Star Fund
WPG Growth & Income
Wright Quality Core Equities

Balanced

Bascom Hill Balanced Fund
CGM Mutual Fund
Dodge & Cox Balanced Fund
Eclipse Balanced Fund
Evergreen American Retirement
Federated Stock & Bond
Fidelity Balanced Fund
Landmark Balanced Fund
Olympic Trust - Balanced
  Income
Pax World Fund
Permanent Portfolio
State Farm Balanced Fund
Twentieth Century Balanced
  Investors
USAA Balanced Portfolio Fund
USAA Cornerstone
Vanguard Wellington Fund

Equity Income

Advantage Income Fund

Alger Income & Growth
  Portfolio
Amana Mutual Fund Trust -
  Income
American Pension Inv - Cap Inc
Mairs & Power Income Fund
Olympic Jr - Equity Income
SAFECO Income Fund
SEI Inst'l Managed - Equity
  Income
Sit New Beginning Income &
  Growth
Stratton Monthly Dividend
T. Rowe Price Equity Income
  Fund
United Service Income
USAA Mutual Income
Vanguard Equity Income Fund
Vanguard Preferred Stock Fund
WPG Dividend Income Fund

Flexible Income

Dreyfus Convertible Securities
  Fund
Fidelity Capital & Income Fund
Fidelity Convertible Securities
  Fund
Founders Equity Income Fund
Janus Flexible Income Fund
Maxus Income Fund
Nicholas Income
SBSF Convertible Securities
USAA Mutual Income
Value Line Convertible Fund
Value Line Income Fund
Vanguard Convertible
  Securities Fund
Vanguard Wellesley Income
  Fund
Wells Fargo Asset Allocation
  (IRA)

Corporate Bond

AARP High Quality Bond Fund
Babson Bond Trust Portfolio L
Babson Bond Trust Portfolio S
Bartlett Capital Fixed Income
  Fund
Bell Atlantic Mutual - Bond
Bernstein Intermediate Duration
Bernstein Short Duration
Berwyn Income Fund
Bond Portfolio for Endowments
Boston Company Managed
  Income
Columbia Fixed Income
  Securities Fund
Counsellors Fixed Income
Crabbe Huson Income Fund
Dodge & Cox Income
Dreyfus A Bonds Plus
Elfun Income Fund
Federated Bond Fund
Fidelity Flexible Bond Fund
Fidelity Intermediate Bond Fund
Fidelity Short-Term Bond
  Portfolio
Financial Bond Shares—Select
  Income
Flex Bond Fund
GE S & S Long-Term Interest
Guardian Bond Fund
Harbor Fund - Bond
Helmsman Income
Legg Mason Inc Trust -
  Investment Grade
Neuberger & Berman Limited
  Maturity Bond Fund
Neuberger & Berman Ultra
  Short Bond Fund
Newton Income Fund
Pimit Low Duration
Pimit Short Term Portfolio
Pimit Total Return
Portico Funds - Bond IMMDEX
Portico Funds - Short-Int Fixed
  Income
Regis-DSI Ltd Maturity
SAFECO Intermediate-Term
  Bond
Scudder Income Fund
Scudder Short Term Bond
SEI Index Funds - Bond Index
SEI Institutional Managed Bond
SEI Institutional Managed-Ltd
  Vol
SIT New Beginning Invest
  Reserve
Stein Roe Income Fund
Stein Roe Intermediate Bond
  Fund
Strong Advantage Fund
Strong Short-Term Bond Fund
T. Rowe Price New Income
  Fund
T. Rowe Price Short Term Bond
  Fund
T. Rowe Price Spectrum Growth
Twentieth Century Long-Term
  Bond
UMB Bond Fund
Vanguard Bond Market Fund
Vanguard Fixed Income
  Investment Grade Bond
Vanguard Fixed Income Short
  Term Bond
Wasatch Income Fund
Weitz Series - Fixed Income

Corporate High Yield

Advantage High Yield Bond
Federated Floating Rate Trust
Federated High Yield Trust
Financial Bond Shares—High
  Yield Portfolio

GIT Income Trust—Maximum Income Portfolio
Northeast Investors Trust
SAFECO High Yield Bond Fund
Strong Income Fund
T. Rowe Price High Yield Fund
Value Line Aggressive Income Trust
Vanguard Fixed Income High Yield Corporate

Government Securities

AARP GNMA & U.S. Treasury Fund
Advantage Government Securities
Benham Target Maturities Trust Series 1995
Benham Target Maturities Trust Series 2000
Benham Target Maturities Trust Series 2005
Benham Target Maturities Trust Series 2010
Benham Target Maturities Trust Series 2015
Benham Target Maturities Trust Series 2020
Benham Treasury Note Fund
Bernstein Government Short Duration
Boston Company Intermediate Term Government
Columbia U.S. Government Securities
Counsellors Intermediate Maturity
Crabbe Huson U.S. Government Income
DFA Five-Year Government Portfolio

Dreman Bond Portfolio
Dreyfus Short Intermediate Government Fund
Dreyfus U.S. Government Bond L.P.
Dreyfus U.S. Government Intermediate
Federated Income Trust
Federated Intermediate Government Trust
Federated Short Intermediate Government Trust
Federated Intermediate Government Trust
Fidelity Government Securities
Financial Bond Shares U.S. Government Portfolio
Founders Government Securities
Gateway Government Bond Plus
GIT Income Trust Government Portfolio
Landmark U.S. Government Inc
Legg Mason U.S. Government Intermediate
Merriman Government Fund
Primary U.S. Government Fund
Reich & Tang Government Securities
Rushmore U.S. Government Intermediate
Rushmore U.S. Government Long Term
Scudder Target Zero Coupon Bond 1995
Scudder Target Zero Coupon Bond 2000
SEI Cash Plus Trust - Intermediate Government
SEI Cash Plus Trust - Short Term Government A
Sit New Beginning U.S. Government Securities

Spartan Government Income
Fund
Spartan Limited Maturity
Government
State Farm Interim Fund
Stein Roe Government Income
Strong Government Securities
T. Rowe Price U.S. Treasury
Intermediate
T. Rowe Price U.S. Treasury
Long-Term
Twentieth Century U.S.
Government
Value Line U.S. Government
Securities
Vanguard Fixed Income Short
Term Federal
Vanguard Fixed Income Long
Term U.S. Treasuries
Vista U.S. Government Income
Wells Fargo Fixed Income (IRA)
WPG Government Securities
Wright Near-Term Bond Fund

Government Mortgage-Backed

Benham GNMA Income Fund
California Investment Trust -
U.S. Gov't
Dreyfus GNMA Fund
Federated GNMA Trust
Fidelity GNMA Portfolio
Fidelity Mortgage Securities
Fund
Lexington GNMA Income Fund
SAFECO U.S. Government
Securities
Scudder GNMA Fund
SEI Cash Plus Trust - GNMA
T. Rowe Price GNMA Fund
Vanguard Fixed Income GNMA
Wright Current Income Fund

Municipal Bond

AARP Insured Tax-Free
General Bond Fund
Babson Tax Free Income Long
Term
Babson Tax Free Income
Portfolio Short Term
Bayshore Tax-Free Fund
Benham National Tax Free
Intermediate
Benham National Tax Free
Long Term
Bernstein Diversified
Boston Company Tax Free -
National
Columbia Municipal Bond Fund
Dreyfus Insured Municipal
Bond
Dreyfus Intermediate Municipal
Bond
Dreyfus Short Intermediate
Tax-Exempt Bond Fund
Dreyfus Tax Exempt Bond Fund
Elfun Tax-Exempt Income Fund
Empire Builder Tax Free Bond
Federated Intermediate
Municipal Trust
Federated Short Intermediate
Municipal Trust
Fidelity Insured Tax-Free
Portfolio
Fidelity Limited Term
Municipals
Fidelity Municipal Bond
Portfolio
Financial Tax Free Income
Shares
General Municipal Bond Fund
Lexington Tax-Exempt Bond
Fund
Neuberger & Berman
Municipal Securities Trust

SAFECO Municipal Bond Fund
Scudder Managed Municipal
  Bond
Scudder Medium Term Tax Free
Scudder Tax Free Target 1993
Scudder Tax Free Target 1996
SEI Tax Exempt Trust -
  Intermediate
Sit New Beginning Tax-Free
  Income Fund
Spartan Municipal Income Fund
Spartan Short Intermediate
  Municipal Fund
State Farm Municipal Bond
  Fund
Stein Roe Intermediate
  Municipals
Stein Roe Managed Municipals
T. Rowe Price Tax Free Income
T. Rowe Price Tax Free Short
  Intermediate
Tax-Exempt Portfolio Limited
  Term
Twentieth Century Tax-Exempt
  Intermediate Term Bond
Twentieth Century Tax-Exempt
  Long Term Bond
United Service Funds—Tax Free
USAA Tax Exempt
  Intermediate-Term
USAA Tax Exempt Short-Term
  Fund
Vanguard Municipal Bond
  Insured Long Term
Vanguard Municipal Bond
  Intermediate Term
Vanguard Municipal Bond Long
  Term
Vanguard Municipal Bond
  Short Term
Vista Tax Free Income
Wright Insured Tax Free

In addition to the funds listed above, many of the management groups have tax-exempt funds for individual states. These funds hold only municipal bonds that are issued by a particular state or Puerto Rico.

Energy /Natural Resources

Neuberger & Berman Selected
  Sections + Energy
T. Rowe Price New Era Fund
Vanguard Specialized Energy

Financial Services

Century Shares Trust
Financial Strategic Financial
  Services

Gold and Precious Metals

Benham Gold Equities Index
  Fund
Financial Strategic Gold
Lexington Gold Fund
Rushmore Precious Metals
  Index
Scudder Gold
United Service World Gold
  Fund
United Services Gold Shares
USAA Gold
Vanguard Specialized Gold &
  Precious Metals

Health Care

Financial Strategic Health
  Sciences
Vanguard Specialized Health
  Care

International Bond

Fidelity Global Bond Fund
Scudder International Bond
Fund
T. Rowe Price International
Bond

International Equity

Babson Stewart Ivory
International
Boston Company International
Counsellors International Equity
DFA Continental Small
Company Portfolio
DFA United Kingdom Small
Company Portfolio
Elfun Global Fund
Evergreen Global Real Estate
Financial Strategic European
Financial Strategic Pacific Basin
Founders Worldwide Growth
Fund
Harbor Fund - International
Helmsman International Equity
IAI International Fund
Ivy International Fund
Japan Fund
Kleinworth Benson
International Equity Fund
Lexington Global Fund
Nomura Pacific Basin Fund
Schroder International Equity
Scudder Global
Scudder International Fund
Stein Roe International Growth
Fund

T. Rowe Price International
Discovery
T. Rowe Price International
Stock Fund
Trustees' Commingled Fund
International Portfolio
United Service European Equity
Fund
USAA International Fund
Vanguard World International
WPG International
Wright International Blue Chip
Equity

Technology

Financial Strategic Technology
T. Rowe Price Science &
Technology
Vanguard Specialized
Technology

Utilities

American Gas Index
Fidelity Select Utilities
Financial Strategic Utilities

Other

Financial Strategic Leisure
PRA Real Estate Securities
United Service Real Estate Fund
Vanguard Specialized Service
Economy

APPENDIX B

Directory of No-Load Mutual Funds

This alphabetical directory provides the addresses and telephone numbers of the mutual fund groups listed in Appendix A (No-Load Mutual Funds—By Investment Objective).

AARP Funds
160 Federal Street
Boston, MA 02110
800-225-2470
800-225-5163

Afuture Fund
617 Willowbrook Lane
West Chester, PA 19382
215-344-7910
800-523-7594

Allegro Growth Fund
P.O. Box 74450
Cedar Rapids, IA 52407
319-366-8400

Armstrong Associates
1445 Ross Avenue LB 212
Dallas, TX 75202
214-720-9101

Advantage Funds
60 State Street
Boston, MA 02109
800-243-8115
800-544-9268

Alger Funds
75 Maiden Lane
New York, NY 10038
800-992-3863

Amana Mutual Fund Trust
101 Prospect Street
Bellingham, WA 98225
206-734-9900
800-728-8762

Babson Funds
2440 Pershing Road
Kansas City, MO 64108
816-471-5200
800-422-2766

Bartlett Capital Trust
36 E. Fourth Street
Cincinnati, OH 45202
513-621-4612
800-800-4612

Bayshore Funds
61 Broadway
New York, NY 10006
212-363-3300
800-237-3113

Beacon Hill Mutual Fund
75 Federal Street
Boston, MA 02110
617-482-0795

Benham Funds
1665 Charleston Road
Mt. View, CA 94043
415-965-8300
800-321-8321

Berwyn Funds
1189 Lancaster Avenue
Berwyn, PA 19312
215-640-4330

Boston Company Funds
One Boston Place
Boston, MA 02108
800-225-5267

Bruce Fund
20 N. Wacker Drive
Chicago, IL 60606
312-236-9160

Bascom Hill Balanced Fund
6411 Mineral Point Road
Madison, WI 53705
608-273-2020
800-767-0300

BB&K Diversa Fund
2755 Campus Drive
San Mateo, CA 94403
415-571-6002
800-882-8383

Bell Atlantic Funds
50 E. Swedesford Road
Frazer, PA 19355
800-527-6644

Bernstein Funds
767 Fifth Avenue
New York, NY 10153
212-756-4097

Bond Portfolio for Endowments
Four Embarcadero Center
San Francisco, CA 94111-4125
415-421-9360
800-325-3590

Brandywine Fund
3908 Kennett Pike
Greenville, DE 19807
302-656-3017
800-338-1597

Caldwell Fund
250 Tampa Avenue West
Venice, FL 34285
813-488-6772
800-338-9477

California Investment Trust
44 Montgomery Street
San Francisco, CA 94104
415-398-2727
800-225-8778

CGM Funds
399 Boylston Street
Boston, MA 02117
617-578-1333
800-345-4048

Columbia Funds
P.O. Box 1350
Portland, OR 97207
503-222-3606
800-547-1707

Copley Fund
315 Pleasant Street
Fall River, MA 02720
508-674-8459
800-424-8570

Crabbe Huson Funds
121 S.W. Morrison
Portland, OR 97204
503-295-0919
800-541-9732

Dodge & Cox Funds
One Sansome Street
San Francisco, CA 94104
415-434-0311

Dreyfus Funds
144 Glenn Curtiss Boulevard
Uniondale, NY 11556
718-895-1206
800-645-6561

Century Shares Trust
1 Liberty Square
Boston, MA 02109
617-482-3060
800-321-1928

Clipper Fund
9601 Wilshire Boulevard
Beverly Hills, CA 90210
213-278-5033
800-776-5033

Concorde Value Fund
5430 LBJ Freeway
Dallas, TX 75240
214-387-8258
800-338-1579

Counsellors Funds
466 Lexington Avenue
New York, NY 10017-3147
800-888-6878
212-878-0600

DFA Funds
1299 Ocean Avenue
Santa Monica, CA 90401
213-395-8005

Dreman Funds
10 Exchange Place
Jersey City, NJ 07302
201-332-8228
800-533-1608

Eclipse Funds
144 E. 30th Street
New York, NY 10016
212-696-4130
800-872-2710

Elfun Funds
P.O. Box 120074
Stamford, CT 06912-0074
203-326-4040
800-242-0134

Evergreen Funds
2500 Westchester Avenue
Purchase, NY 10577
914-694-2020
800-235-0064

Fam Value Fund
P.O. Box 310
Cobleskill, NY 12043
518-234-4393

Federated Funds
Federated Investors Tower
Pittsburgh, PA 15222-3779
412-288-1900
800-245-2423

Fiduciary Funds
222 E. Mason Street
Milwaukee, WI 53202
414-226-4555
800-338-1579

Flex Funds
P.O. Box 7177
Dublin, OH 43017
800-325-3539

Founders Funds
3033 E. First Avenue
Denver, CO 80206
303-394-4404
800-525-2440

Empire Builder Tax Free Fund
230 Park Avenue
New York, NY 10169
212-309-8400
800-872-2710

Fairmont Fund
1346 S. Third Street
Louisville, KY 40208
502-636-5633
800-262-9936

Fasciano Fund
190 S. LaSalle Street
Chicago, IL 60603
800-338-1579
312-444-6050

Fidelity Funds
82 Devonshire Street
Boston, MA 02109
800-544-6666

Financial Funds
P.O. Box 2040
Denver, CO 80201
800-525-8085

Fontaine Capital Appreciation
111 S. Calvert Street
Baltimore, MD 21202
301-385-1591
800-247-1550

Fremont Funds
50 Fremont Street
San Francisco, CA 94105
415-768-6225

Gabelli Funds
P.O. Box 1634
New York, NY 10163
212-490-3670
800-422-3554

Gateway Trust
400 Technecenter Drive
Milford, OH 45150
800-354-6339

General Funds
144 Glenn Curtiss Boulevard
Uniondale, NY 11556
718-895-1396
800-242-8671

GIT Funds
1655 Fort Myer Drive
Arlington, VA 22209
800-336-3063

Harbor Funds
One Seagate
Toledo, OH 43666
800-422-1050

Hummer Funds
175 W. Jackson Boulevard
Chicago, IL 60604
312-431-1700
800-621-4477

Jamestown Fund
6630 W. Broad Street
Richmond, VA 23230
804-288-0404

Galaxy Funds
3512 Silverside Road
Wilmington, DE 19810
302-478-6945
800-441-7379

GE S&S Funds
P.O. Box 120074
Stamford, CT 06912-0074
203-326-4040
800-242-0134

Gintel Funds
Greenwich Office Park
Suite 6
Greenwich, CT 06831
203-622-6400
800-243-5808

Greenspring Fund
Quadrangle Village of Crosskey
Baltimore, MD 21210
301-435-9000

Helmsman Funds
111 E. Wisconsin Avenue
Milwaukee, WI 53202
800-338-4345

Ivy Funds
40 Industrial Park Road
Hingham, MA 02043
617-749-1416
800-235-3322

Janus Funds
100 Fillmore Street
Denver, CO 80206
303-333-3863
800-525-3713

Japan Fund
160 Federal Street
Boston, MA 02110
800-225-2470
800-225-5163

Kleinworth Benson
International Equity
200 Park Avenue
New York, NY 10166
212-687-2515
800-237-4218

Lazard Special Equity
345 Park Avenue
New York, NY 10154
212-326-6656
800-854-8525

Lepercq-Istel Fund
1675 Broadway
New York, NY 10019
212-698-0749
800-338-1579

LMH Fund
P.O. Box 830
Westport, CT 06881
800-522-2564
800-422-2564

Mathers Fund
100 Corporate North
Bannockburn, IL 60015
708-295-7400
800-962-3863

Meridian Fund
60 E. Sir Francis Drake Boulevard
Larkspur, CA 94939
415-461-6237
800-446-6662

Kaufmann Fund
17 Battery Place
New York, NY 10004
212-344-2661

Landmark Funds
6 St. James Avenue
Boston, MA 02116
617-432-1679

Legg Mason Funds
P.O. Box 1476
Baltimore, MD 21203
301-539-3400
800-822-5544

Lexington Funds
P.O. Box 1515
Saddle Brook, NJ 07662
201-845-7300
800-526-0057

Mairs & Power Funds
W2062 First National
Bank Building
St. Paul, MN 55101
612-222-8478

Maxus Funds
3550 Lander Road
Pepper Pike, OH 44124
216-292-3434

Merriman Funds
1200 Westlake Avenue, North
Seattle, WA 98109
206-285-8877
800-423-4893

Muhlenkamp Fund
P.O. Box 598
Wexford, PA 15090
412-935-5520

National Industries Fund
1801 Century Park East
Los Angeles, CA 90067
213-277-1450

Neuwirth Fund
140 Broadway
New York, NY 10005
212-504-4000
800-225-8011

Nicholas Funds
700 Water Street
Milwaukee, WI 53202
414-272-6133

Northeast Investors Funds
50 Congress Street
Boston, MA 02109
617-523-3588
800-225-6704

Pax World Fund
224 State Street
Portsmouth, NH 03801
603-431-8022
800-767-1729

Perritt Capital Growth
680 N. Lakeshore Drive
Chicago, IL 60611
312-649-6940
800-338-1579

Mutual Funds
51 John F. Kennedy Parkway
Short Hills, NJ 07078
201-912-2100
800-448-3863

Neuberger & Berman Funds
342 Madison Avenue
New York, NY 10173
212-850-8300
800-877-9700

Newton Funds
411 E. Wisconsin Avenue
Milwaukee, WI 53202
800-242-7229

Nomura Pacific Basin Fund
180 Maiden Lane
New York, NY 10038
212-208-9300
800-833-0018

Olympic Funds
800 W. Sixth Street
Los Angeles, CA 90017
213-623-7833

Permanent Funds
P.O. Box 5847
Austin, TX 78763
800-531-5142
512-453-7558

Pimit Funds
P.O. Box 9000
Newport Beach, CA 92658
714-760-4884
800-443-6915

Pine Street Fund
140 Broadway
New York, NY 10005
212-504-4000
800-225-8011

PRA Real Estate Securities Fund
44 Montgomery Street
San Francisco, CA 94104
415-296-8700

Reich & Tang Funds
100 Park Avenue
New York, NY 10017
212-370-1110

SAFECO Funds
SAFECO Plaza
Seattle, WA 98185
206-545-5530
800-426-6730

Schafer Value Fund
210 Carnegie Center
Princeton, NJ 08540
609-936-1200
800-338-1579

Scudder Funds
160 Federal Street
Boston, MA 02110
800-225-2470
800-225-5163

Sentry Fund
1800 North Point Drive
Stevens Point, WI 54481
715-346-6000
800-533-7827

Portico Funds
207 E. Buffalo Street
Milwaukee, WI 53202
414-287-3808
800-228-1024

Regis-DSI Funds
P. O. Box 2600
Valley Forge, PA 19482
215-648-6000
800-662-7447

Rushmore Funds
4922 Fairmont Avenue
Bethesda, MD 20814
301-657-1500
800-343-3355

SBSF Funds
45 Rockefeller Plaza
New York, NY 10011
212-903-1258
800-422-7273

Schroeder International Equity Fund
787 Seventh Avenue
New York, NY 10019
212-841-3830
800-845-8406

Selected Funds
1331 Euclid Avenue
Cleveland, OH 44115-1831
800-553-5533

Sherman Dean Fund
6061 NW Expressway
San Antonio, TX 78201
512-735-7700
800-247-6375

Sit Funds
90 S. Seventh Street
Minneapolis, MN 55402
612-334-5888
800-332-5580

Sparton Funds
82 Devonshire Street
Boston, MA 02109
800-544-6666

Stein Roe Funds
P.O. Box 1143
Chicago, IL 60690
800-338-2550

Stratton Funds
610 West Germantown Pike
Plymouth Meeting, PA 19462
215-941-0255
800-634-5726

Tax-Exempt Portfolio
82 Devonshire Street
Boston, MA 02109
800-544-6666

Tocqueville Fund
1675 Broadway
New York, NY 10019
212-698-0858
800-225-6258

Twentieth Century Funds
P.O. Box 419200
Kansas City, MO 64141-6200
816-531-5575
800-345-2021

Sound Shore Fund
100 Park Avenue
New York, NY 10017
203-629-1980

Special Portfolio
Box 64284
St. Paul, MN 55164
612-738-4000
800-800-2638

Stralem Fund
405 Park Avenue
New York, NY 10022
212-888-8123

T. Rowe Price Funds
100 East Pratt Street
Baltimore, MD 21202
301-547-2308
800-638-5660

Thompson, Unger & Plumb Fund
8201 Excelsior Drive
Madison, WI 53717
608-831-1300

Trustees' Funds
Vanguard Financial Center
Valley Forge, PA 19842
215-648-6000
800-662-7447

UMB Funds
2440 Pershing Road
Kansas City, MO 64108
816-471-5200
800-422-2766

United Services Funds
P.O. Box 29467
San Antonio, TX 78229-0467
800-873-8637

USAA Funds
USAA Building
San Antonio, TX 78288
800-531-8181

Valley Forge Fund
P.O. Box 262
Valley Forge, PA 19481-9990
215-688-6839
800-548-1942

Value Line Funds
711 Third Avenue
New York, NY 10017
212-687-3965
800-223-0818

Vanguard Funds
P.O. Box 2600
Valley Forge, PA 19482
215-648-6000
800-662-7447

Variable Stock Fund
361 Whitney Avenue
Holyoke, MA 01040
413-732-7100

Vista Funds
156 W. 56th Street
New York, NY 10019
800-62-CHASE

Volumetric Fund
87 Violet Drive
Pearl River, NY 10965
914-623-7637
800-541-3863

Wasatch Funds
68 S. Main Street
Salt Lake City, UT 84101
801-533-0777
800-345-7460

Weitz Funds
9290 W. Dodge Road
Suite 405
Omaha, NE 68114
402-391-1980

Wellesley Fund
P.O. Box 2600
Valley Forge, PA 19482
215-648-6000
800-662-7447

Wellington Fund
P.O. Box 2600
Valley Forge, PA 19482
215-648-6000
800-662-7447

Wells Fargo Funds
111 Sutter Street
San Francisco, CA 94104
415-396-7690
800-572-7797

William Blair Funds
135 S. LaSalle Street
Chicago, IL 60603
312-236-1600

Windsor Funds
P.O. Box 2600
Valley Forge, PA 19482
215-648-6000
800-662-7447

Wright Funds
P.O. Box 1559
Boston, MA 02104
617-482-8260
800-225-6265

WPG Funds
One New York Plaza
New York, NY 10004
212-908-9532
800-223-3332

44 Wall Street Funds
26 Broadway
New York, NY 10004
212-248-8080
800-543-2620

APPENDIX C

Worksheets

To make your life simpler and more productive as a mutual fund investor, we are including four worksheets to help you analyze funds and keep a record of purchases, sales and distributions. You will also find a sample letter for corresponding with funds on any changes in your program or redemptions you may want to make.

FUND ANALYSIS

When considering funds for purchase or evaluating funds you already own, it is helpful to compare the key data on each fund in one simple format. In making such a comparison, examine funds with the same investment objective together, such as growth funds, balanced funds, income funds and so on. The fund analysis worksheet will enable you to evaluate important factors, such as the size of each fund; the percentage annual yield; the amount by which expenses reduce annual return; the total return over one-, five- and ten-year periods; and the trend in dividend payments.

PURCHASE AND SALE RECORD

You will have all the information you need for income tax purposes on the statements provided by the mutual fund companies. However, it is convenient to have this data in one place so that you can see at a glance a complete picture of your investment history in the funds you own. Reporting capital gains and losses to the IRS is simple and can be done from this form when you take all distributions in cash. But when the automatic reinvestment option is used, it can get more complex, especially if you make partial redemptions from time to time. Remember, each year you must report for tax purposes all dividend and capital gains distributions, whether taken in cash or reinvested. All such reinvested distributions are considered new investments and increase the cost of the total shares you own. When you sell, be sure to include the cost of all shares purchased by automatic reinvestment in calculating any profit or loss.

RECORD OF DISTRIBUTIONS

This record provides a convenient way to keep track (in a single place) of the periodic distributions made by each fund. From the record, you can easily determine your monthly income from mutual funds and can perhaps see months where income is too low and should be supplemented by purchasing other funds or by setting up an automatic withdrawal plan.

MULTIPURPOSE FORM LETTER TO FUNDS

Some transactions can be effected by a simple toll-free telephone call to your fund. Use the telephone whenever possible. But there will be many times when written instructions are required, and this sample letter can help you in those cases. You can actually use this form, or a copy of it, for most needs. When corresponding, write to the fund you own by name, sending it to the address listed on the transaction statement the fund sends you. Don't forget to include your account number as it appears on the statement. Also, be sure that your correspondence is signed by each and every owner of the fund if it is jointly owned. It may be that the signatures must be guaranteed (not notarized). This can be done by your local bank. Ask your fund if this is required before mailing the letter.

Fund Analysis

Primary Objective _____

Date of Analysis _____

Facts To Consider	Funds To Compare				
Total Assets (000,000)					
Net Asset Value Per Share					
Last 12 Months Distribution					
Investment Income					
Percent Yield on Net Asset Value					
Expense Ratio					
Total Return Percent Last 12 Months					
Last 5 Years					
Last 10 Years					
Dividends Paid Last 5 Years					
19__					
19__					
19__					
19__					
19__					

Purchase and Sale Record

Fund	Number of Shares	Date Acqred Mo./Day/Yr.	Amount Invested	Date Sold Mo./Day/Yr.	Sale Proceeds	Gain (Loss)

Record of Distributions

Income Received During 19__	Fund	Fund	Fund	Fund	Fund	Fund
Jan.						
Feb.						
Mar.						
Apr.						
May						
June						
July						
Aug.						
Sept.						
Oct.						
Nov.						
Dec.						
Total						

Multipurpose Form Letter to Funds

To: _____   Date: _____

      _____

      _____

      _____

From: _____

      _____

      _____

      _____

RE: Acct. # _____

Please take the following action concerning this account:

_____ Liquidate the entire above-mentioned account.

_____ Liquidate only _____ shares.

_____ Liquidate enough shares to send a check for _____.

_____ Liquidate all attached shares only.

_____ Change my income option to:

      ___ Reinvest dividends and capital gains

      ___ Reinvest capital gains and pay dividends in cash

      ___ Pay dividends and capital gains in cash

_____ Other: _____

_____

_____

_____

_____

_____

_____   _____
Owner   Joint Owner

APPENDIX D

Dow Jones Industrial Average, 1929 to 1991

The Dow Jones Industrial Average is simply an average of 30 well-known industrial stocks, predominantly of the so-called blue chip variety. The continuity of this average is maintained by changing the divisor whenever there is a substitution, stock split or stock dividend that changes the average by five points or more.

Year	12/31 Close	Dividend	Year	12/31 Close	Dividend
1929	248.48	12.75	1947	181.16	9.21
1930	164.58	11.13	1948	177.30	11.50
1931	77.90	8.40	1949	200.13	12.79
1932	59.93	4.62	1950	235.41	16.13
1933	99.90	3.40	1951	269.23	16.34
1934	104.04	3.66	1952	291.90	15.48
1935	144.13	4.55	1953	280.90	16.11
1936	179.90	7.05	1954	404.39	17.47
1937	120.85	8.78	1955	488.40	21.58
1938	154.76	4.98	1956	499.47	22.99
1939	150.24	6.11	1957	435.69	21.61
1940	131.13	7.06	1958	583.65	20.00
1941	110.96	7.59	1959	679.36	20.74
1942	119.40	6.40	1960	615.89	21.36
1943	135.89	6.30	1961	731.14	22.71
1944	152.32	6.57	1962	652.10	23.30
1945	192.91	6.69	1963	762.95	23.41
1946	177.20	7.50	1964	874.13	31.24

Year	12/31 Close	Dividend	Year	12/31 Close	Dividend
1965	969.26	28.61	1979	838.74	50.98
1966	785.69	31.89	1980	963.99	54.36
1967	905.11	30.19	1981	875.00	55.65
1968	943.75	31.34	1982	1,046.54	54.14
1969	800.36	33.90	1983	1,258.64	56.33
1970	838.92	31.53	1984	1,211.57	59.83
1971	890.20	30.86	1985	1,546.67	62.05
1972	1,020.02	32.27	1986	1,895.95	67.04
1973	850.86	35.33	1987	1,938.83	71.20
1974	616.24	37.72	1988	2,168.57	79.53
1975	852.41	37.46	1989	2,753.20	103.00
1976	1,004.65	41.40	1990	2,633.66	103.70
1977	831.17	45.84	1991	3,168.83	95.18
1978	805.01	48.52			

GLOSSARY

account registration form   Accompanies a prospectus and is completed by a prospective investor to provide a mutual fund with account name, address, social security number and other pertinent data.

account statement   A statement sent by a mutual fund to each shareholder at least annually. It indicates the shareholder's registration, account number, tax ID number and shares owned. It also lists the account activity and a summary of dividends and distributions paid during the statement period.

accumulation plan   An arrangement whereby an investor makes regular purchases of mutual fund shares in large or small amounts.

adviser   See **investment management company.**

asked price   The price at which the buyer may purchase shares of a mutual fund (the net asset value per share plus the sales charge, if any).

average cost–double category   Permits calculation of investment cost by averaging costs of shares held for short-term with those held long-term.

average cost–single category   Permits calculation of investment cost by averaging the cost of all shares regardless of the holding period.

back-end load   A redemption fee charged to an investor in certain mutual funds when shares are redeemed within a specified number of years after purchase.

balanced fund A mutual fund that at all times holds bonds and/or preferred stocks in varying ratios to common stocks to maintain relatively greater stability of both capital and income.

bank draft plan A periodic cash investment made through a shareholder's checking account via bank drafts, for the purpose of regular share accumulation.

bid price The price at which the holder of open-end mutual fund shares may redeem those shares. In most cases it is the net asset value (NAV) per share. For closed-end fund shares, it is the highest price then offered for stock in the public market. It may be more or less than the net asset value (NAV) per share.

blue chip The common stock of large, well-known companies with a relatively stable record of earnings and dividend payments over many years.

blue-sky laws Laws of the various states regulating the sale of securities, including mutual fund shares, and the activities of brokers and dealers.

bond A security representing debt. A loan from the bondholder to the corporation.

break-point In the purchase of mutual fund shares, the dollar value level at which the percentage of the sales charge becomes lower. A sales charge schedule typically contains five or six break-points.

broker A person in the business of effecting security purchase and sale transactions for the accounts of others. He or she receives a commission for those services.

call (1) The exercise by an issuer of its right to retire outstanding securities. (2) An option contract that gives the holder the right to purchase a particular security from another person at a specified price during a specified period of time.

call price The price that an issuer of preferred stock or bonds must voluntarily pay to retire such securities.

capital (1) The assets of a business, including plant and equipment, inventories, cash and receivables. (2) The financial assets of an investor.

capital gains Profits realized from the sale of securities.

capital gains distribution A distribution to shareholders from net capital gains realized by a mutual fund on the sale of portfolio securities.

capital growth   An increase in the market value of securities.

cash equivalent   Includes U.S. government securities, short-term commercial paper and short-term municipal and corporate bonds and notes.

cash position   Includes cash plus cash equivalent minus current liabilities.

certificates of deposit (CDs)   Interest-bearing certificates issued by commercial banks or savings and loan associations against funds deposited in the issuing institutions.

check-writing privilege   A service offered by some mutual funds (particularly money market funds) permitting shareholders of such funds to write checks against their fund holdings. The holdings continue to earn dividends until the checks are cashed.

closed-end fund   An investment company with a relatively fixed amount of capital and whose shares are traded on a securities exchange or in the over-the-counter market.

commercial paper   Short-term, unsecured promissory notes issued by corporations to finance short-term credit needs. The maturity at the time of issuance normally does not exceed nine months.

common stock   A security representing ownership of a corporation's assets. The right to common stock dividends comes after the requirements of bonds, debentures and preferred stocks. Shares of common stock generally carry voting rights.

common stock fund   A mutual fund whose portfolio consists primarily of common stocks. Such a fund may at times take defensive positions in cash, bonds and other senior securities.

common trust fund   A mutual fund organized and administered by a bank or trust company for the benefit of its own trust account customers.

contractual plans   A type of accumulation plan under which the total intended investment amount is specified in advance, with a stated paying-in period and provision for regular monthly or quarterly investments. A substantial amount of the applicable sales charge is deducted from the first year's payments.

controlled affiliate   A mutual fund company in which there is any direct or indirect ownership of 25 percent or more of the outstanding voting securities.

convertible securities   Securities carrying the right to exchange the security for other securities of the issuer (under certain conditions). This normally applies to preferred stock or bonds carrying the right to exchange for given amounts of common stock.

corporate (master or prototype) retirement plan   A plan and trust agreement that qualifies for special tax treatment available to a corporation or other organization whereby it can purchase the shares of a fund for the benefit of plan participants.

current assets   In a mutual fund, includes cash plus cash equivalent less current liabilities.

current liabilities   Obligations due within one year or less.

custodian   The bank or trust company that holds all cash and securities owned by a mutual fund. It may also act as transfer agent and dividend disbursing agent but has no responsibility regarding portfolio policies.

dealer   A person or firm who buys and sells securities to others as a regular part of its business. Mutual fund shares with a sales charge are usually purchased through dealers.

debenture   A bond secured only by the general credit of a corporation.

declaration of trust   A document that identifies a specific fund and declares that it is being held in trust for a specified beneficiary.

defensive stock   A stock that is expected to hold up relatively well in declining markets, because of the nature of the business represented.

direct purchase fund   A mutual fund whose shares are purchased directly from the fund at a low charge or at no charge. The investor deals directly with the fund, rather than through a broker or dealer.

discount   The percentage below net asset value (NAV) at which the shares of a closed-end mutual fund sell.

distributions   Dividends paid from net investment income and payments made from realized capital gains.

diversification   Investment in a number of different security issues for the purpose of spreading and reducing the risks that are inherent in all investing.

diversified investment company   A company that, under the Investment Company Act, in respect to 75 percent of total assets, has invested not more than 5 percent of its total assets in any one company and holds not more than 10 percent of the outstanding voting securities of any one company.

dividend   A payment from income on a share of common or preferred stock.

dollar cost averaging   A method of automatic capital accumulation that provides for regular purchases of equal dollar amounts of securities and results in an average cost per share lower than the average price at which purchases have been made.

dual-purpose fund   A type of closed-end mutual fund that is designed to serve the needs of two distinct types of investors: (1) those interested only in income and (2) those interested only in possible capital gains. It has two separate classes of shares.

earnings   In respect to common stock, net income after all charges (including preferred dividend requirements) divided by the number of common shares outstanding.

equity securities   The securities in a corporation that represent ownership of the company's assets (generally common stocks).

exchange privilege   The right to exchange the shares of one open-end mutual fund for those of another under the same fund group at a nominal charge (or at no charge) or at a reduced sales charge. For tax purposes, such an exchange is considered a taxable event.

expense ratio   The proportion that annual expenses, including all costs of operation, bear to average net assets for the year.

fiduciary   A person who has legal rights and powers to be exercised for the benefit of another person.

first in, first out (FIFO)   An accounting method for determining cost basis that assumes the first shares sold are the first shares purchased.

fixed-income security   A preferred stock or debt instrument with a stated percentage or dollar income return.

forward averaging   A special tax treatment available for certain lump-sum distributions from qualified retirement plans.

forward pricing   The pricing of mutual fund shares for sale, redemption or repurchase at the next computed price after the receipt of an order. Pricing is usually done at 4:00 P.M., when the New York Stock Exchange closes.

front-end load   A sales fee charged investors in certain mutual funds at the time shares are purchased.

government agency issues   Debt securities issued by government-sponsored enterprises, federal agencies and international institutions. Such securities are not direct obligations of the Treasury but involve government guarantees or sponsorship.

growth stock   A stock that has shown better-than-average growth in earnings and is expected to continue to do so as a result of additional resources, new products or expanded markets.

hedge fund   A mutual fund that hedges its market commitments by holding securities it believes are likely to increase in value and at the same time is "short" other securities it believes are likely to decrease in value. The only objective is capital appreciation.

incentive compensation   A fee paid to an investment adviser that is based wholly or in part on management performance in relation to specified market indices.

income   The total amount of dividends and interest received from a fund's investments before deduction of any expenses.

income fund   A mutual fund whose primary objective is current income.

individual retirement account (IRA)   A tax-saving retirement program for individuals, established under the Employee Retirement Income Security Act of 1974.

inflation   A persistent upward movement in the general price level of goods and services that results in a decline in the purchasing power of money.

investment adviser   See **investment management company**.

investment company   A corporation or trust through which investors pool their money to obtain supervision and diversification of their investments.

Investment Company Act of 1940   A federal statute enacted by Congress in 1940 for the registration and regulation of investment companies.

investment management company   An organization employed to advise the directors or trustees of an investment company in selecting and supervising the assets of the investment company.

investment objective   The goal of an investor or investment company. It may be growth of capital and income, current income, relative stability of capital or some combination of these aims.

investment policies   The means or management techniques that an investment manager employs in an attempt to achieve his or her investment objective.

investment trust   See **investment company**.

junior securities Common stocks and other issues whose claims to assets and earnings are contingent on the satisfaction of the claims of prior obligations.

Keogh plan A tax-favored retirement program for self-employed persons and their employees. (It is also known as an H.R.10 plan or self-employed retirement plan.)

letter of intention A pledge to purchase a sufficient amount of mutual fund shares within a limited period (usually 13 months) to qualify for the reduced selling charge that would apply to a comparable lump-sum purchase.

leverage The effect of using borrowed money or other senior capital to magnify changes in the assets and earnings available for junior issues.

liquid Assets that are easily converted into cash or exchanged for other assets.

living trust A trust instrument made effective during the lifetime of the creator, in contrast to a testamentary trust, which is created under a will.

load See **selling charge**.

low-load indicates that the sales fee charged to investors in certain mutual funds is approximately one percent to three percent of the amount invested.

management company See **investment management company**.

management fee The charge made to an investment company for supervision of its portfolio. It frequently includes various other services and is usually a fixed or reducing percentage of average assets at market value.

management record A statistical measure, expressed as an index, of what an investment company management has accomplished with the funds at its disposal.

money market fund A mutual fund whose investments are in short-term debt securities, designed to maximize current income with liquidity and capital preservation.

money purchase pension plan A retirement program to which a percentage of the earnings of participating employees is contributed each year. The pension amount received by a participant at retirement depends on the amount contributed and earnings achieved on the funds over the period of participation.

municipal bond fund A mutual fund that invests in diversified holdings of tax-exempt securities, the income from which is exempt from federal taxes.

mutual fund See **open-end investment company**.

National Association of Securities Dealers (NASD) An organization of brokers and dealers in the over-the-counter securities market that administers rules of fair practice and rules to prevent fraudulent acts for the protection of the investing public.

net asset value (NAV) Total resources at market value less current liabilities.

no-load fund See **direct purchase fund**.

offering price See **asked price**.

one-party trust An arrangement where the creator of a trust (the settler) is also named as the trustee.

open account An account whereby a shareholder, by virtue of his or her initial investment in a fund, automatically has reinvestment privileges and the right to make additional purchases.

open-end investment company An investment company whose shares are redeemable at any time at approximate net asset value. In most cases, new shares are offered for sale continuously.

option A right to buy or sell specific securities at a specified price within a specified period of time.

optional distribution A payment from realized capital gains or investment income that an investment company shareholder may elect to take in either cash or additional shares.

payroll deduction plan An arrangement between a fund and an employer under which money is deducted from the employee's salary to purchase shares in the fund.

pension plan A retirement program based on a definite formula that provides fixed benefits to be paid to employees for their lifetime upon the attainment of a stated retirement age.

pension rollover The opportunity to take distributions from a qualified pension or profit-sharing plan and, within 60 days from the date of distribution, reinvest them in an individual retirement account (IRA).

performance See **management record**.

performance fund An investment company that appears to emphasize short-term results and that usually has had rapid turnover of portfolio holdings. It may also refer to any fund that has had an outstanding record of capital growth.

periodic payment plan   See **accumulation plan**.

portfolio   The securities owned by an investment company.

portfolio turnover   The dollar value of purchases and sales of portfolio securities, not including transactions in U.S. government obligations and commercial paper.

preferred stock   An equity security, generally carrying a fixed dividend, whose claim to earnings and assets must be paid before common stock is entitled to share.

premium   The percentage above net asset value (NAV) at which the shares of a closed-end fund trade.

profit-sharing retirement plan   A retirement program to which a percentage of the profits of a company is contributed each year for the benefit of the plan's participants.

prospectus   The official document that describes the shares of a new issue. This document must be provided to each purchaser, under the Securities Act of 1933. It applies to closed end funds only when new capital is raised.

prototype retirement plan   A retirement plan document that has been determined by the Internal Revenue Service to satisfy the requirements in the tax laws for qualified retirement plans.

Prudent man rule   The law governing the investment of trust funds in those states that give broad discretion to the trustee.

put   An option contract that gives the holder the right to sell a particular security to another person at a specified price during a specified period of time.

qualified plans   Retirement plans that meet the requirements of Section 401(a), 403(a) or 403(b) of the Internal Revenue Code or the Self-Employed Individuals Tax Retirement Act.

redemption in kind   Redemption of investment company shares for which payment is made in portfolio securities rather than cash. It is permissible for many mutual funds and tax-free exchange funds.

redemption price   See **bid price**.

reduction-of-tax-basis dividend   Payment by an investment company that is nontaxable as current income but must be used to reduce the tax cost of the shares.

registered investment company An investment company that has filed a registration statement with the Securities and Exchange Commission (SEC) under the requirements of the Investment Company Act of 1940.

registration statement Document containing full and accurate information that must be filed with the Securities and Exchange Commission (SEC) before new securities can be sold to the public.

regular account A lump-sum purchase of mutual fund shares without provision for automatic dividend reinvestment or planned periodic additions or withdrawals.

regulated investment company An investment company that has elected to qualify for the special tax treatment provided by Subchapter M of the Internal Revenue Code.

reinvestment privilege A service offered by most mutual funds and some closed-end investment companies through which dividends from investment income may be automatically invested in additional full and fractional shares.

repurchases Refers to the voluntary open-market purchases by closed-end funds of their own shares. In mutual funds, the term represents shares taken back at their approximate net asset value (NAV).

right of accumulation The application of reduced sales charges to quantity purchases of mutual fund shares made over an extended period of time.

sales commission See **selling charge**.

Securities and Exchange Commission (SEC) An independent agency of the U.S. government that administers the various federal securities laws.

selling charge An amount that, when added to the net asset value (NAV) of mutual fund shares, determines the offering price. It covers commissions and other costs and is generally stated as a percentage of the offering price.

senior securities Notes, bonds, debentures or preferred stocks. These issues have a claim ahead of common stock as to assets and earnings.

shareholder experience A measure of the investment results that would have been obtained by an actual mutual fund shareholder.

It is usually expressed in terms of a hypothetical $10,000 investment.

short sale   The sale of a security that is not owned (but is borrowed) in the hope that the price will go down so that it can be repurchased at a profit.

simplified employee pension (SEP) plan   A retirement plan whereby employers can make deductible contributions to individual retirement accounts (IRAs) established for their employees.

specialty or specialized fund   An investment company concentrating its holdings in specific industry groups.

specific shares   An accounting method for determining cost basis that lets the investor identify the specific shares being sold.

sponsor   Usually refers to the principal underwriter of an investment company's shares.

statement of additional information   Contains more complete information than is found in a prospectus and is on file with the Securities and Exchange Commission.

swap fund   See **tax-free exchange fund**.

tax-free exchange fund   An investment company organized to permit investors holding individual securities selling at appreciated prices to exchange such securities for shares of the fund, without payment of capital gains tax.

total return   A statistical measure of performance reflecting the reinvestment of both capital gains and income dividends.

treasury bill   A non-interest-bearing security issued by the U.S. Treasury and sold at a discount, with a maturity of one year or less.

turnover ratio   The extent to which an investment company's portfolio (exclusive of U.S. government obligations and commercial paper) is turned over during the course of a year.

12b-1 fee   The fee charged by some funds, permitted under a 1980 Securities and Exchange Commission rule (for which it is named), to pay for distribution costs such as advertising or for commissions paid to brokers.

uncertificated shares   Fund shares credited to a shareholder's account without the issuance of stock certificates.

unrealized appreciation or depreciation   The amount by which the market value of a portfolio's holdings exceeds or falls short of its cost.

U.S. government securities   Various types of marketable securities issued by the U.S. Treasury, consisting of bills, notes and bonds.

volatility   The relative rate at which a security or fund share tends to move up or down in price as compared with some market index.

voluntary plan   An accumulation plan without any stated duration or specific requirements. Sales charges are applicable to each purchase made.

warrant   An option to buy a specified number of shares of an issuing company's stock at a specified price, usually for a specified time.

withdrawal plan   An arrangement provided by many mutual funds by which an investor can receive periodic payments in a designated amount, which may be more or less than the actual investment income.

yield   Income received from investments, usually expressed as a percentage of the market price.

yield to maturity   The rate of return on a debt security held to maturity. Both interest payments and capital gain or loss are taken into account.

INDEX